The Path of th
MYSTIC LOVER

MW00379530

◆

The Path of the
MYSTIC LOVER

Baul Songs of Passion and Ecstasy

◆

BHASKAR BHATTACHARYYA

◆

Edited by
Nik Douglas

◆

Illustrated by
Penny Slinger

Destiny Books
Rochester, Vermont

Destiny Books
One Park Street
Rochester, Vermont 05767

Library of Congress Cataloging-in-Publication Data
Bhattacharyya, Bhaskar.
    The path of the mystic lover : Baul songs of passion and ecstasy / by Bhaskar Bhattacharyya ; edited by Nik Douglas ; illustrated by Penny Slinger.
        p.   cm.
    Bibliography: p.
    Includes index.
    ISBN 0-89281-019-X
    1. Bauls—Prayer-books and devotions—History and criticism.   2. Bauls—Hymns—History and criticism.   I. Douglas, Nik.   II. Slinger, Penny, 1947–
III. Title.
    BL1284.86.B47 1992
    294. 5'512—dc19   86-19780
                                                                                CIP

Printed and bound in the United States

10 9 8 7 6 5 4 3 2 1

Text design by Virginia L. Scott

Destiny Books is a division of Inner Traditions International, Ltd.

Distributed to the book trade in the United States by American International Distribution Corporation (AIDC)

Distributed to the book trade in Canada by Book Center, Inc., Montreal, Quebec

Man's wandering heart
Is the Uncatchable

Song of Chandi Gosai

CONTENTS

FOREWORD

There is something very special and appealing about the Bauls, something significant and lasting. Once one's life has been touched by them, they can never be forgotten. Having heard their thrilling songs of passion and ecstasy and experienced their charismatic and spontaneous manner, there can be no turning away. Though most Bauls are deeply religious, they rarely follow any fixed doctrine; instead, they take the most ordinary or mundane subjects and express them as mystic teaching. They have no time for intellectualization, preferring to express fundamental truths directly and poetically. Above all, Bauls are "knowers," free from dogma. And they are fun to be with.

About twenty-four years ago, early in my search for the Tantric knowledge of secret India, I happened to spend Christmas in Shantiniketan, West Bengal. This small university town, founded by the great poet and artist Rabindranath Tagore as a "campus under the trees," was alive with expectancy. Bauls were coming to town and everyone was talking about them.

Tagore had "discovered" the Bauls in the early part of this century and encouraged them to share their inspirational songs with his students. Tagore took many of his poetic themes from the Baul lifestyle and was especially influenced by the songs of Lalan Fakir, several of which are included in this collection. Over the years an annual Baul festival or *Mela* was created in Tagore's honor, attracting minstrels and their families from all parts of Bengal.

I had a brief encounter with two Bauls the year before while making the documentary film "Tantra."* The film crew, some musicians, friends, the

---

*Tantra: Indian Rites of Ecstasy, now re-released in video by Mystic Fire, ISBN 1-56176-217-2. A film by Nik Douglas, produced with Mick Jagger and Robert Fraser.

Tantric master Durga Das, and myself were traveling by private bus through Bengal when we were suddenly told to stop by Durga Das. Though we could see no obvious reason to do so, we complied. Several minutes later two Bauls came out of the forest, entered the bus, and prostrated themselves before Durga Das. With tears streaming down their faces, they sang several songs to him, who, it turned out, had instructed them several years before. On completing their songs, they once again touched his feet and went on their way. As we continued our journey, I wondered how Durga Das knew they were in the vicinity and about the meaning of their songs, which had seemed so filled with spirituality and joy.

I knew who the Bauls were, since the long-playing record album *The Bauls of Bengal* had recently been released on the CBS label and had impressed me greatly. At that time I could hardly imagine how Bauls created such exciting sounds and was intrigued by the translated lyrics and the photos on the album cover. In a way their music could be compared to the innovative, dynamic, and spontaneous style of guitarist Jimi Hendrix, yet the lyrics reminded me of the mystic poetry of Khalil Gibran. When I looked at the producer's credit, I was astonished to read the name Robert Zimmerman, who was none other than the popular folksinger Bob Dylan.

As the Shantiniketan Baul festival got underway it became evident that something special was about to take place—something quite different from the ordinary Hindu religious gathering. Everyone I met in Shantiniketan asked me what I thought of the Bauls. Had I heard their music or listened to their "dirty" songs? What did I think of their eccentric dress and crazy manner? Did I know that they smoked ganja and sometimes lived in cremation grounds? That they traveled about in couples or groups, living together for a while, and then drifted apart? And did I, an Englishman, think that they should be allowed to act so outrageously?

A friend of mine, a professor at the Shantiniketan university, whispered to me that some years back an American poet named Allan Ginsberg had visited Bengal and spent time with the Bauls; he speculated that perhaps this was the cause of his peculiar "beat" poetry. A Muslim rickshaw driver told me that he knew there were saints among the Bauls who could heal by mere touch. And the Hindu sweeper in the house where I was staying told me he would not be available to work while the Bauls were in town since he felt obligated to spend time helping with their campsite; he added that this might aid him to get a better rebirth the next time around. He also said there was a

Baul lady who liked him and who might be willing to favor him. A middle class Indian friend of mine seemed very embarrassed about the presence of the Bauls and suggested that I forgive their wild ways since they were not typically Hindu, and probably resulted from ignorance.

I must admit that the feedback I was getting on the Bauls made me more interested in them. When I went to the Baul camp I saw that a temporary shelter had been erected, with a performance area, living quarters, and a catering section. The atmosphere reminded me of the arrangements for an open-air rock concert.

The first group of Bauls that I encountered beckoned me over with smiling faces, offering tea, sweets, food, fruit, and a chillum pipe. They made space for me among them and though we had only a few words in common, there was little problem in communication. I soon realized that I had found some good friends and that my experiences with them would turn into something worthwhile, something meaningful and lasting.

I decided to record some of their songs and learn as much as I could about their way of life. I had brought my camera and was delighted that, unlike members of most Indian religious cults, Bauls actually enjoyed having their photos taken and were intrigued by the recordings that I made. Little did I know then that a book, a record album, and a documentary film series on them would eventually be released as a direct result of my visit.

The 1968 Christmas Baul festival at Shantiniketan is indelibly fixed in my psyche. For several days and nights I was transported into another reality, a place full of spirit and love. I became "adopted" as a Baul, with Baul "brothers and sisters" and a Baul "father." And I shared the taste of the ecstasy they were experiencing. Drawn as I was into their midst, I found myself exhilarated by their convention-free lifestyle and the unique atmosphere surrounding them. When the festival was over, everyone just packed up and moved out, in twos and threes, in different directions. As I said goodbye to my new-found friends, I was told I could join up with them right away or, if I had things to do, I could meet them in two weeks at neighboring Jaidev Kenduli, the birthplace of one of their principal Gurus.

I did not manage to keep that appointment and at times have regretted not following up on their generous invitation to roam with them. Instead, I returned to my responsibilities and to my books and studies. Later I continued my pilgrimage for several years through India's sacred places, met many teachers, and then returned to England. I have been making return trips to India and Southeast Asia ever since.

Early in 1976 I met Bhaskar Bhattacharyya in London and we soon found that we shared a common interest in both the Bauls and the Tantric traditions of India. I lent Bhaskar my tapes recorded at the Shantiniketan Baul festival and he responded with an out-of-print book compilation of Baul songs in Bengali. We found ourselves listening to the latest Bob Dylan album "John Wesley Harding," which had several Bauls featured on the front cover, who looked remarkably like Native Americans. We noted that there were a number of Baul record albums in the stores, and we even saw notices that some Bauls would soon be touring in Europe and America. So Bhaskar and I discussed doing a book together, to put across the authentic Baul way of life to the reading public.

I had also recently met the English surrealist artist Penny Slinger and she became very excited by the Baul project. She told me of a particularly mystical psychedelic experience she had while listening to a Baul record. It's as if these songs were originally "seen" in the mind's eye, and the poems and songs are descriptions of these images. Penny was quick to unravel the visual nature of most of our Baul songs. It soon became evident that the very paradoxical nature of so many of the songs made them ideally suited as subjects for surrealistic renderings.

Penny was also able to help Bhaskar and me craft the translated songs into English poetic form. The three of us carefully considered how to achieve our goal of an esoteric yet accessible and visual work. We decided to put together as comprehensive a collection on songs as possible, selected so we could explore and comment on their special Tantric meanings; each song would be illustrated in a collagelike way. We hoped we would be able to put out a record album to coincide with the finished book. We felt that the combination of Bhaskar's knowledge of Bengali and his connection to the Tantric tradition, combined with Penny's abilities in surrealistic poetry and collage, my own knowledge of Bauls and Tantra, and my experience in publishing could lead to a worthwhile result. I agreed to finance additional research in India and to see if I could get a publisher interested.

Bhaskar returned to India and spent several months with Bauls, collecting new material and seeking answers to his many questions. The Bauls welcomed him and offered to cooperate with us not only on our book project but also on a documentary film series and a record album.* Over the next few years, this book, the television series† and the record album began to take shape.

Penny and I moved to America and continued with other publishing projects. Bhaskar visited us there and in time we were able to finalize our collection of eighty-four Baul songs with commentaries. Finally we found a publisher, but the high cost of doing color separations of the color collages that were intended to illustrate the songs, and the somewhat esoteric and seemingly bizarre nature of the material— deemed uncommercial—led to further delays. Bhaskar took up a full-time career as a producer/researcher of movies and Penny and I moved to the Caribbean.

Finally it was decided that, no matter what, the book must come out

---

*Le Chant des Fous, a double album by Le Chant du Monde, Paris, France.

†"Bauls of Bengal," produced by Georges Luneau for Antennae-2 by Les Films Cinemare, Paris, France.

and that the most practical way of illustrating the songs inexpensively would be with drawings. Penny took up this awesome challenge and over the course of another year completed eighty-four half-tone pencil drawings, one for every song. Each page has been designed so that text and image complement each other, with the commentaries placed with each song. Bhaskar's background on the Bauls, his account of their Way of Love, and his very personalized preface are thorough and informative. Many of these topics appear in print here for the first time.

I am particularly pleased that this book is finally finished and published. There are several important aspects to the Baul lifestyle that distinguish them from other obscure Indian cults. Bauls come from both Hindu and Muslim backgrounds. They serve an important function by bringing esoteric teachings to the masses while also providing social commentary and entertainment. Their role is something akin to the calypso singers of the West Indies, but generally the message of Baul songs is deeper and more meaningful.

There are no organized or definitive Baul scriptures. All teachings are transmitted directly, mostly through the songs, but also through debate and informal discussion. Above all, Baul teachings are both practical and delightful. They can lead to self-realization, the highest human achievement.

Baul sexual practices are especially interesting. Basing their teachings on authoritative yogic and Tantric viewpoints, Bauls elevate the sexual act to the highest form of sacrament. Though the sexual-yogic practices of the Bauls are kept quite private, in their songs Bauls use erotic language and sexual puns to create an atmosphere that is charged with sensuality, eroticism, and is potentially "initiatory." In modern India the word "Baul" has become associated with loose speech and lewd behavior. It is hoped that this book will help set the record straight.

The apparently bizarre nature of some Baul secret sexual practices can be understood on many different levels. As with all Tantric teachings there is a deliberate trend toward unconventionality and experimentation, together with a tendency toward mysticism. I am sure there are great truths to be learned from understanding how Baul sexual-yogic techniques work, since if these were not practical and worthwhile, Bauls would have set them aside long ago. It is only in recent years that we in the West have come to understand something of the true potential of the human body. While we now look to psychological or hormonal explanations for some of our behavior, Baul yogis and yoginis forge ahead. Their knowledge of "solar" and "lunar" currents within the body, the different internal secretions, polarities, tides,

xiv
◆
THE PATH OF THE
MYSTIC LOVER

and our sacramental substances, is of great worth. I have no doubt that in time much of what seems bizarre in Baul sexual-yogic practice will be explainable in Western scientific terms. In the meantime, Bauls should be given the benefit of any doubt and viewed as experienced travelers along a paradoxical path.

I hope the readers of this book will experience as much delight and fascination in the Bauls as I have. The sheer poetry of the eighty-four songs and the wonderful illustrations that go with them speak for themselves. Perhaps English-speaking Bauls or Western musicians will be inspired to perform or record some of them. Recently (1992) Allan Ginsberg told me his 1963 visit to India was largely because of his hearing about the Bauls. It is reassuring to know that in the twentieth century there are still ecstatic minstrel-poets roaming the countryside and cities. No matter what madness the rest of mankind creates, Bauls are here to stay and have much to teach. Here is another of India's secret treasures, a signpost on the Path of the Mystic Lover. To those who wish to "Catch the Uncatchable," I say, read this sign with loving care!

I would like to thank everyone who has helped bring this project to completion, and to Bauls everywhere for exemplifying a precious ideal.

Nik Douglas
Anguilla, West Indies, 1992

PREFACE

A memory lingers from my childhood. Time has fuzzed the details, but the colors still glow just as brightly. It has rooted itself deep within my consciousness and in a curious way has become the symbol of freedom and spiritual liberation. Two crazy-looking minstrels came into the courtyard of our house in Calcutta and began to sing the most wonderful and enchanting songs. It was almost magical; they plucked their one-stringed instruments, beat their drums, and danced as they sang. Being only four years old, I could only understand a few words, but lack of comprehension did not seem to matter. These pied pipers in many-colored robes stole my heart. Having glimpsed ecstasy through the tiniest of keyholes, my heart yearned for more.

Many years passed and I "grew up." The childlike memory hid behind many dreams, surfacing occasionally. In its whirlwind wandering, the heart desperately searched to taste the essence of that passion. To my mule-consciousness this fantasy was like a juicy carrot. But a fool knows no reason, only the craving of his heart. In the course of time many other symbols of freedom arose but somehow they were never complete, for there always seemed to be a motive, a forced effort to try to shape and order what was essentially without reason or form. Only the image of the wandering madman seemed to suggest an effortless consciousness, a liberated spirit that cared not for the ways of heaven or hell, let alone earth, and yet loved with deep compassion. I looked around for many years, in India and in the West, for someone or something that would represent this fantasy, a mirror that would reflect the unseeable. Sometimes it almost seemed possible and other times graspable, but inevitably this passion escaped.

One day I went to pay my respects to Pandit Gopinath Kaviraj in Benares. I mentioned to Baba (as I called him) that it was the time of the year when the Bauls gathered at Jaydev Kenduli, in Bengal, for a three-day festival. He became very enthusiastic and encouraged me to go. Baba said that the Bauls were true mystics and that if I went to Kenduli I would find out more about Tantra and Radha-Krishna Lila. He also added, "There you will find the Man of your Heart." I had over the years learned a little to unravel some of Baba's enigmatic sayings, but I had no idea that the expression "Man of your Heart" was anything more than a poetic expression for a soulmate. With his blessings, I left Benares with Subodh, a friend of mine.

It would be very difficult to express the effect that my sojourn with the Bauls had on me, if only because to this day I am still left intoxicated. What I had imagined to be only a romantic flight of fantasy suddenly appeared real. There really were madmen and madwomen, *khepas* and *khepis,* whose spirits danced effortlessly. There was a spontaneity, an impulsive passion that filled the air. Among the holy, sensual pleasures abounded. This was at first confusing because in my travels with various sects of sadhus, I had noticed either a total ascetic detachment from sensual pleasures or a hypocritical moral stance. While people talked of God, they forgot humans. I had been studying Sanskrit in Benares, the bastion of Hindu orthodoxy; slowly an insidious puritanism was creeping up on me. My brahmin heritage was raising its proud head. The rebel in me was copping out. My heart yearned for freedom, but my mind seemed to opt for "reason" and "tradition."

Not only was this experience with the Bauls a fulfillment of a dream, but it gave rise to innumerable other dreams. Sitting in the burning-ghats at Jaydev, I seemed to lose myself and become another. A part of me awoke and stirred upon hearing Radha's lament, her passionate abandon of self for her beloved. I tried to catch that elusive, fleeting sound of Krishna's flute. There was an old Bhairavi (a Tantric woman ascetic) there called Ganga-Ma, who spoke to the little image of Kali that she had in her hut. Sometimes she spoke to Kali as a mother and sometimes as a daughter. I asked her, "Mother, why is this passion so fleeting? I hear the sound of the flute, but when I try and concentrate on it, it vanishes." The old lady, with an adolescent glint in her eye, smiled naughtily and said, "One cannot hold on to Love, one can only play with it. The 'Man of your Heart' is waiting to play with you." Baba's words before I left Benares came home to me.

I returned to Benares, swirling in a sea of music, inspiration, and images. There were a million questions I wanted to ask Baba. What did all those riddles mean, those enigmatic verses that I did not understand but that nevertheless inspired me? It felt like running after smoke to look for fire. Baba was very pleased to see me excited with a positive yearning to know. In his inimitable way, he explained some of the symbols and pointed in the direction I should go if I wanted to find out more.

Again that memory slid into the unconscious, and though from time to time I felt moved and inspired by the songs of the Bauls, it never really took hold on me. I just did not persevere enough for my desire. I was careless with my love.

In the summer of 1976, during a visit to England, I met Nik Douglas, an old friend of mine whom I had known in India. A writer of some repute and a practicing Tantric, beneath his multifaceted existence, Nik had a passion for the mystic Lila of the yogis. As my visit in England lengthened I saw more of Nik, and of Penny Slinger, an established surrealist artist who at that time was working with Nik on a series of collages depicting various Tantric concepts. As we all shared many common interests and had a deep involvement with Indian spiritual paths, it was not surprising that a continual stream of project ideas would manifest each time we met. But they were more than just "creative raps" around the fireside on cold winter evenings.

Both Nik and I shared a fascination for the *sadhu* traditions of India, and often we would exchange anecdotes, reflections, and information about the various sadhus (renunciates) that we had come across. Like me, Nik felt instinctively attracted to the Bauls and had for some time contemplated a project involving them. It became obvious that we should collaborate on an illustrated book about the Bauls. I began by translating a few Baul songs. Some were collected by Upendranath Bhattacharyya for his authoritative work *Banglar Baul O Baul Gan,* some were from my own collection, and some were from live tapes that Nik had recorded a few years earlier at a Baul festival in Bengal. Previously, when I had listened to Baul songs, I had not paid close attention to the meaning behind the words, even though I was aware of their mystical roots. I had been content merely to enjoy the various sentiments. From now on everything would be serious. In order to write about the songs, I would first have to understand them and all their multifaceted levels of meaning.

I began to spend a considerable amount of time in the library at the School of Oriental and African Studies, University of London, plowing my way through any articles, books, or manuscripts that had even a remote connection with the Bauls. Though there was much information regarding the classical traditions, philosophies, and Bengali literature and history (all of which have shaped Baul thought and poetry), there was hardly any material that dealt exclusively or directly with my interest. I suspected that the key to unraveling Baul songs would be in Sahajiya literature. With the exception of a half-dozen Sahajiya texts, most of the other information was peripheral. The scholars either were interested purely in the aesthetics of Baul and Sahajiya songs or viewed them strictly from an orthodox Vaishnava stance. (For further background on the Sahajiya Vaishnava tradition, see pages 24–30.) Since doctoral theses on philosophy must draw on reliable information, sources, and the written tradition, it is not surprising that there was so little about Sahajiya Vaishnavism. It would not be unfair to say that scholasticism is not a strong feature of the Bengali Sahajiyas. However, Upendranath Bhattacharyya's book on the Bauls is an exception, for in it he displays not only erudition but genuine empathy with the Bauls as well. This is hardly surprising. He spent many years with the Bauls, carefully documenting information and collecting well over a thousand songs.

I felt the need to go back to Bengal and spend time with the Bauls—watching, learning, and playing. From my experiences with sadhus in India I had learned that the written word is only the tip of the iceberg of knowledge, as far as Indian mysticism is concerned; that the vast treasure house of esoteric knowledge lies hidden deep within seemingly ordinary people. I remembered the advice Baba had once given before I set off for the Kumbha Mela Festival: "Try and avoid the large gatherings and performances. Stay with the humble and you will find much wealth." I was sure that my questions would be answered in Bengal.

Few events are accidents, and even in my chaotic world things happen with uncanny coincidence. Nik suggested that I go to India and offered to finance the trip. I went to Bengal and stayed there for four months. I traveled, with my friend Debdas Baul, moving from one Baul *akhara* to another and meeting many Bauls, who have since become very close friends. I felt I had arrived home.

The Bauls say that the best treasures are found within one's home; theirs certainly are. The richness of their tradition expressed itself to me on every face, at every moment, in every place. I was awed, and still am, by the vast body of knowledge that their people collectively possess. Hardly anything is written down; it is all passed from guru to disciple, from one friend to another.

Esoteric teachings are often labeled "secret knowledge," thereby implying an elitist and xenophobic nature. Certain cults that have megalomaniacal tendencies often hide their secular ambitions behind a thin facade of spirituality. For cults that have love as the core of their mysticism, how can it be so? Is

Debdas Baul, traveling companion and close personal friend of the author. Photo by Bhaskar Bhattacharyya.

◆

not love an all-embracing experience that opens doors, that reveals and expresses itself without fear or prejudice? Baul teachings are only secret insofar as they are not advertised; for the eager the doors to the treasure house are always open. Many of the Bauls I met and befriended were illiterate. But far from being uneducated they displayed a tremendous storehouse of verbal knowledge; thousands of songs (Baul, Sahajiya, orthodox Vaishnava, Tantric, and even Brahminical), sacred scriptures, mythologies, secular literature, and folklore—all committed to memory.

If the music of the Bauls had seemed enchanting, then they themselves were even more so. In the poverty-ridden villages, among the sick and the hungry, the old and the young, the jewels shone. There was never any hesitation in answering the most intimate questions. At first my questions were forced, too intent; I was impatient to have all the answers for my book. But the Bauls follow the Sahaj path, the effortless, spontaneous, and playful way of the "madman." Where, when, and how the gems come out has little to do with an intellectually logical process and more to do with emotional inspiration and outbursts. As I learned to play the game, a mixture of teasing, provoking, and loving, the essence slowly started to flow. Bauls often say that unless one pokes into a fruit, its juice will never flow out.

We would sit around the dim oil lamps in the evening, sometimes singing and other times discussing spiritual and worldly topics or simply playing the fool. Slowly the Baul tradition started to reveal itself. What I began to discover was more, much more, than what I had ever imagined, even in my wildest dreams. It wasn't just the flood of information; there was also a native intelligence that seemed to be able to deal and play with the vast array of emotions. The Baul tradition allows for dreams as well as the understanding of perennial and immediate problems. Not only was my mind dazed, my heart began to reverberate to ancient echoes. Sometimes it was almost embarrassing, as when old women, looking so traditional and pious, started to talk about sexual passion and practices in the most personal and direct terms. This was a considerable contrast to most of my previous experience in India, where sexual topics are rarely discussed between men and women.

During those first four months my roots sunk deep among the Bauls and other sadhus of Bengal. The family became bigger. Since that time, I have returned to Bengal several times, sharing the experiences of my brothers and sisters among the Bauls. For a writer, such an involvement can sometimes be a problem, because the more one involves oneself, the more subjective one gets.

Most of what I have learned from the Bauls has come straight from the oral tradition, where verification of information and sources is not always possible. Inconsistency is an inherent problem in oral traditions. While this may be frustrating for scholars, it is rarely a problem for those who are embedded into the tradition. I have tried to give a panoramic view, an approximation at best, of the Bauls' history, lifestyle, music, religious beliefs, and practices. There will inevitably be inconsistencies, and occasionally inaccuracies; for that I apologize. The Bauls themselves not only are aware of

*The author (far left) with his "extended family,"
a group of Bauls.*

◆

inconsistencies, paradoxes, and contradictions but actually encourage contrary opinions. At every level there is a dialogue between the believer and the skeptic. The Baul tradition is a living tradition that has been handed down from one generation to another, changing according to whims of times, situations, and people.

I feel I should apologize to the Muslim Bauls and Fakirs for being unable to present more information about their Sufi heritage. I have not spent a great deal of time with them, only occasionally meeting them at fairs and festivals and in wayside encounters. Though they, too, have fascinated me, my natural inclinations have steered me toward the Vaishnava Bauls. There are two reasons for this. First, because of my own spiritual orientation

I am attracted to the central motif of the Vaishnava Bauls, the love-dalliance of Radha and Krishna, and to the Tantric and yogic practices that the Bauls employ to realize their mystic ideal. Second, the Muslim Baul and Fakir communities are almost exclusively male-dominated, and the playful sensuality between men and women that one witnesses among Vaishnava Bauls seems absent.

I have felt it inappropriate to expound the religious beliefs of the Muslim Bauls without having learned much from the oral tradition. Though there are many differences of terminology, religious observances, and social milieu between the Hindu and Muslim Bauls, there is a common spirit that unites them. Both respect the essential truths of Islam and Hinduism, and yet discard those aspects that separate the two religions. If human beings are the common denominator in every religion, then why not love humanity? I was filled with hope and optimism from my encounters with the Muslim Bauls and Fakirs, and of their relationship with the Hindu Bauls. There is much communal tension in India between Muslims and Hindus, often resulting in violent local warfare. The fanatic elements in both communities, under the guise of religion, spread intolerance and hatred. Their orthodox religious mentors are usually motivated by political gains and a distorted sense of religious duties. The blind follow the evil to the edge of the cliff. Within this context the way of the Bauls appears like a shining ray of hope. It is not uncommon in Bengali villages to see the heretics of both religions participating together. The Fakir will sing songs of Radha and the Vaishnava Baul will praise the merciful Allah. There has always been a strong bond among the downtrodden in Bengal. Tolerance is much greater than among the educated middle classes. But the poor peasant and the worker have little time or expressive ability for their sentiments. Their bards, the Fakirs and the Bauls, do it for them.

Despite so many varied expressions, there is a unifying spirit, a strong identity, that defines the Bauls. While their outer garb of theology, philosophy, and metaphysics is pertinent, indeed important, it is their insatiable passion for life, love, and laughter that is the source of the spirit. But, just as many people are disappointed when they go to India in search of enlightened mystics, only to come across people with the usual human virtues and vices, so might the traveler who goes to Bengal in search of the "sensuous madman" be disappointed. What makes the Bauls unique is that they are ordinary people with an extraordinary and rich inner life. They are not poets or musicians who live in gilded palaces, or ascetics who live in remote Himalayan caves;

they are quite simply people who go through the usual hardships, the inevitable lot of the poor, and yet rise above it. In an insane world where man creates so much suffering, is it a wonder that the Bauls, who give so much joy, are known as "crazies"? In those timeless moments when the outer sheath of suffering falls aside, they catch the Uncatchable.

Many people have helped in the writing, editing, and compiling of this book. I cannot extend enough thanks to Nik Douglas and Penny Slinger for inspiration, support, editorial work, and many hours of warm companionship. Without them it is doubtful whether the book would have been written. I am also very grateful to my parents for bearing my whims with so much patience and offering much financial and moral help. I cannot express enough gratitude to Helen Coles for her tireless and devoted help in editing and typing the many drafts. Having spent several months with the Bauls herself, she inspired many fresh visions. I would also like to thank Deepak Majumdar for the many enlightening hours in the company of the Bauls. I thank Georges Luneau, who very kindly asked me to work with him on a series of films about the Bauls for French television, and for the use of some of his photographs. I also thank my publisher, Ehud Sperling, for having faith and enthusiasm in the project. Finally, it is to all of the Bauls that I extend my greatest debt of gratitude. There are, however, a few whom I would like to thank particularly: Debdas Baul, for more than generous warmth and love, and for companionship on the road; Kanai, the boatman who ferried me across many rivers; Jaya Khepa, the ultimate mystic rascal, to whom nothing is sacred except love; Raotara Khepa Baba, who is reputed to be 113 years old, for the childlike naughtiness in his eyes; Subal Das and Sundari, for many enchanting hours; Chintamani, a grandmother who teased like an adolescent; Radharani Dasi, for many hours of intense discussions; little Chaya and Karttik, two young Bauls who moved mountains; Gour Khepa and Vishwanath Das, for all the surreal lunacy; lastly, Ramananda Das, who vanished into thin air one day, the epitomy of the Baul spirit.

Bhaskar Bhattacharyya
New Dehli, India, 1992

Part One

◆

THE BAULS

THE MAD MINSTRELS OF BENGAL

*B*engal is a land of rivers. The Ganges, the Brahmaputra, and others with their many tributaries flow down from the Himalayas through broad plains to the Bay of Bengal. In the scorching heat of summer, the land is parched and only the major rivers contain any water. But when the monsoon comes, the rivers burst forth in flood, sweeping away mud houses, inundating rice fields, turning villages into vast swamplands.

The Bengali peasants know the moodiness of the rivers only too well. They are born beside them, live with them, and in death their remains are cast upon them. Like the land of their birth, the Bengalis are a study in contrasts. By temperament they are volatile and highly emotional. While they can be prudish, orthodox, and conventional, they can also be rebellious, sacrilegious, and politically radical. At times parochial and provincial, they yet have a reputation as restless adventurers.

Deeply rooted in this rural society are the Bauls—minstrels who wander the Bengali countryside singing ecstatically of the "Way of Love." The Bauls not only are among the most inspired musicians of India, but are also a devout—though unconventional—mystical religious sect.

With their simple instruments (chiefly string and percussion), they perform at sacred shrines and temples, in the courtyards of palatial mansions, at fairs and festivals, on trains, under the trees, and among the mud huts of villages—anywhere, anytime. Sometimes they sing and dance simply for their own pleasure—yet even then they are rarely without an audience. Gradually a crowd gathers around the strange-looking musicians in multicolored garments. A child, an old woman, a vegetable vendor, a peasant on his way to the fields—all pause for a moment of respite from their daily toil to enjoy the fervor of the Bauls' singing and the freedom and spontaneity of their poetry.

The rural folk feel a kinship with these minstrels, for like them the Bauls are largely poor and illiterate and mostly come from the lower strata of Hindu and Muslim society. To the poor, the old, and the sick, their poignant songs offer the richness of spiritual joy in the midst of poverty, the healing balm of faith in the midst of suffering. It is easier for them to accept this consolation from a poor minstrel in tattered clothes than it would be from an urbane, learned, high-caste soothsayer.

Wherever the Bauls perform, they arouse extreme emotions. There is a saying in the Birbhum district of West Bengal: "A mad wind blows hearing the sound of the Baul's lute." But while their songs make some people mad with joy, others become mad with outrage. For the Bauls do not console the complacent with spiritual flattery. Their songs goad and provoke, charm and tease, shock and amuse with their often enigmatic language, irreverent metaphors, and erotic imagery. And while they declare the bliss of spiritual experience, they openly ridicule the bigotry and hypocrisy of orthodox religion.

Though devout believers, Bauls are nonconformists who reject the outer husk of religion with its elaborate rituals, dogmas, scriptures, institutions, and displays of piety. Not content to tread the straight and narrow path prescribed by the religious establishment, they have chosen the wide and open road to divine ecstasy. Their Way of Love knows no limitations; it is the all-embracing faith in which rich and poor, exalted and humble, young and old, male and female are all equal participants.

In a society bound by strict traditions, rigid class or caste distinctions, and puritanical morality, it is no wonder that many regard Bauls with scorn and outrage. Their ways are different, socially and religiously, from those of both mainstream Hindus and Muslims. Bauls do not believe in the "idol worship" or the authority of the brahmins and sacred texts of Hinduism; nor do they subscribe to the strict moral codes and observances of Islam.

> *Hindus bicker;*
> *Muslims are deceitful.*
> *Says Duddu:*
> *"I have left all this,*
> *Knowing full well!"*
> *song 7*

The faith of the Bauls is deep-seated, rooted not in sectarian beliefs but in a secular spirit of freedom and joy. While they respect, and often integrate, the beliefs of other religious cults, they disdain the profane aspects that dominate most traditional religious lifestyles. The Bauls are fully aware that most organized religions have little to do with spirituality and more to do with pragmatic material gain. They are not afraid to voice their opinion even in socially precarious situations.

Dinabandu Das Baul and Debdas Baul in Tarapith. Photo by Bhaskar Bhattacharyya.

Once I witnessed a display of the Bauls' outspoken irreverence in the village of Tarapith. I was sitting with a group of them near the sacrificial fire in front of the main Tantric shrine dedicated to the goddess Tara. Set among *charnel* (burial) grounds and wooded land, where many Tantrics practice their magical rites in houses made of human skulls and bones, Tarapith has a strangely fascinating atmosphere—a curious mixture of tranquility and violence, of mysticism and superstition, of spiritual fervor and religious hypocrisy. Here, as at most Tantric shrines in Bengal, there is always a steady stream of people who come in search of blessings or the absolution of sins. They generally bring animal or vegetable offerings and have a brahmin priest perform a sacrificial fire ritual for them. On this occasion, a family was sitting around the fire while the priest recited mantras, poured libations, rang bells, and offered fruits and grains into the fire. The Bauls were singing among themselves, when one of them stood up and began to mock the priest's rituals in a melodious and poetic form:

> The brahmin sits down to worship
> And with his bells, clangs away.
> His Tantras and mantras have no use,
> For in the end
> He puts the grains and fruits in a cloth
> And runs away.

The priest was incensed but did not respond, as he could not interrupt the ritual. Yet when the ritual was over, sure enough, he tied the remaining grains and fruits (his fee for performing the ritual) into a red cloth and hurried away.

Orthodox Muslims and Hindus are understandably infuriated by the Bauls' insolence—especially when they hear a singer impudently mock their traditions while at the same time borrowing religious metaphors from their sacred scriptures.

The irregular family life and customs of the Bauls are also disturbing to many. Partly owing to their itinerant lifestyle, Baul husbands and wives frequently separate, and there is some degree of promiscuity. Moreover, their spiritual practices involve sexual yoga, sometimes performed by partners who are not married to each other.

These characteristics of the Bauls—along with their exotic appearance, their custom of smoking of *ganja* (marijuana), and their often bizarre behavior—explain why many people consider them mad. In fact, the word "Baul" means "madcap," and the Bauls themselves refer to each other as *khepa*, meaning "wild," "mad," or "frenzied." Yet the Bauls' madness is not that of the self-deluded or the deranged. It is born of spiritual restlessness, a craving of the soul for the intoxication of divine love. Lost to the ways of the world, the Bauls are ecstatics, weeping for joy, crying out in bliss, dancing and whirling about as they pour out their songs of the heart:

> I have lost my mind.
> I don't know

In what it is lost,
Or why it is in such Bliss.

song 3

Despite their "madness," the Bauls have been tolerated in India; for rigid and puritanical though it may be, Hindu society traditionally accommodates religious diversity. And no doubt the Bauls have become more widely admired by the educated middle class since the nineteenth century when the great Bengali poet Rabindranath Tagore declared his enthusiastic appreciation for their music, poetry, and philosophy.

But perhaps most significant is the power and beauty of the Bauls' songs, and their ability to charm and intoxicate even the most critical of audiences. Even though they express spirituality in unorthodox terms, the Bauls are basically sincere in their religious devotion. People who understand this are able to accept them for what they appear to be—entertaining religious "jesters." After all, only the fool is permitted to ridicule the king!

THE MUSIC OF THE BAULS

While the Bauls' music is unique, it cannot be entirely separated from that of northern India or Bengal. It follows the same melodic modes and rhythmic patterns as northern Indian classical music, but with less variety and technical embellishment. It has much in common with other light classical music and folk music of northern India, as well as with the music of the Sufis, who came to India from the Middle East. However, indigenous elements are found among the older Baul singers and can be noted especially in the typical devotional songs heard at Baul gatherings.

Their Musical Instruments

The most common and perhaps best-loved instrument of the Bauls is the *ektara* ("one string"). At its simplest, it consists of a sound box made of an

empty tin can, and a split bamboo stick with a steel string running from the bottom of the can to the top of the bamboo, where the string is tuned on a wooden key. Most Bauls graduate from this simple instrument to a more sophisticated ektara made of wood or, preferably, a dried gourd. However, I once met a very old Baul, sick and almost blind, who said that after years of using "fancy" instruments, he had taken up his tin can again because he wanted to return to his "original innocence."

The ektara is often accompanied by a drum called a *baya* or *dugi*, which is tied around the waist at the player's side. One hand plays the ektara while the other beats on the dugi. The traditional dugi is a clay bowl, about seven inches in diameter, with a hide stretched across it. It is a smaller version of the bass drum of the *tabla*.

The two basic instruments of Baul music: a dugi (left) and an ektara. Photo by Bhaskar Bhattacharyya.

◆

Most popular among the Bauls' audiences is a two-stringed instrument known as the *goba* or, as the Bauls call it, the *gabgubi*, an onomatopoeia reflecting the hollow, reverberating sounds it produces. It is also known variously as *Ananda lahiri* ("waves of bliss"), *Gopi-yantra* ("instrument of the Gopis"), and *khamak*, a Persian term that may point to the instrument's origin. The sound box of the goba is a wooden cylindrical drum about nine or ten inches high and five inches in diameter. Two loose strings, formerly made of gut but now more often made from badminton strings or fishing line, are tied to the hide at the base of the drum at one end and to a small brass bowl at the other. The goba player holds the drum between the inner arm and the side of the chest, while gripping the brass bowl with the same hand. By tensing the strings and plucking them with a wooden plectrum held in the other hand, the player can produce a wide range of notes. The goba provides both melody and rhythm, and expresses the surging intensity unique to Baul music.

The pure melody instrument of the Bauls is the *dotara,* which means "two strings," even though the instrument has four. It is a folk lute very similar to those found in other parts of India, Afghanistan, Iran, and Turkey. Some Muslim Bauls play the *sarinda,* a three-stringed bowed instrument that probably originated in the Middle East.

A few Bauls play a small hand drum called a *dubki.* Often, when Bauls are singing at Hindu gatherings, they are accompanied by a double-sided drum, the *khol.* For dancing, Bauls wear bells, called *ghunghur* if worn around the ankles and *nupur* if worn over the foot. Small brass cymbals known as *kartal* are usually played by women.

Occasionally one hears Baul music accompanied by the common bamboo flute, which strictly speaking is not a Baul instrument, though it is not entirely out of character with their music. One instrument that is totally alien to the itinerant ways of the Bauls, yet which one hears more and more frequently nowadays, is the hand-pumped harmonium. This is a hybrid instrument borrowed from the Indian middle classes, who in turn inherited it from Europe. However, it is a convenient instrument with which to standardize pitch and scale. In practice, Bauls will play virtually anything—even sticks, stones, and pots!

The Enigmatic Language of Their Songs

The often peculiar and riddle-bound language of most Baul songs adds to their image as madmen. Palm trees growing in the ocean, the sky clad in rags, mice tunneling under a house—odd phrases such as these bewilder most listeners, though many realize that there are sane explanations for the insane images. First, since mystical experiences do not necessarily conform to the logical order of our immediately perceivable world, sometimes the only means of verbal expression is through analogy. Second, like other mystical cults, Bauls have had to veil the essentially sexual nature of their mysticism from the more orthodox public to avoid abuse and scorn. Bauls call this topsy-turvy world *Ultadesh,* the "inverted country."

The enigmatic language of Indian mysticism is called *sandhya* or *sandha bhasa.* The former means "twilight language" and the latter "intentional language." Twilight is a time of transformation, when night suddenly becomes day or day suddenly becomes night. Similarly, in twilight language, the apparent meaning of a word or phrase changes once one learns its hidden meaning. In intentional language, a word or phrase may be interpreted in several ways; the same phrase has one meaning for the public and another, esoteric meaning for the initiate.

An example of twilight language is the phrase "Frogs eat the snake's head" (song 68). Such a statement seems preposterous, for we know that frogs are the snake's prey. But to Bauls, the frog represents the *yoni,* the female sex organ, and the snake the *lingam,* the male organ. The phrase thus refers to the sexual act.

An example of intentional language is a statement about *rasa:* "Uncooked, it becomes sour" (song 31). The word "rasa" literally means "liquid," and in the context of the song it refers to milk, which is cooked in the preparation of a type of Indian sweetmeat. In its esoteric sense, however, rasa refers to the sexual fluids and to erotic passion in general.

The Bauls as Performers

The humblest Baul minstrels eke out a living in the villages singing with the barest of musical accompaniment in exchange for offerings of rice and lentils. They occasionally supplement their income from the sale of crops (if they have any) or charitable offerings from their neighbors. Such Bauls, though the majority, are rarely in the public eye. Their music is simple and untouched by classical or popular influences.

Other performing Bauls are professional musicians who vie with each other for musical supremacy and who are ever on the lookout for more prestigious and lucrative opportunities. These Bauls are often very exotic-looking, wearing assorted beads, colorful scarves, and patchwork robes. The young ones are precocious, mischievous, lovable rogues who display strong individuality; the older ones never really lose their youthful enthusiasm and playfulness.

Middle-class Bengalis often organize musical programs for various reasons—for religious celebrations, fund-raising galas, annual parties at factories, or whatever seems like a good excuse for a gathering. For the Bauls, these programs usually pay fairly well as folk singers' fees go. They attract large crowds whose sole desire is to be entertained and who think of the Bauls as "just a bunch of villagers with good voices." Such audiences have little patience for traditional country tunes, let alone metaphysical nuances, accustomed as they are to the sugary lyrics and razzmatazz cacophony of modern Indian film music. The Bauls who sing at these functions must compromise their musical standards by playing shorter, simpler, and more saccharine songs. But true to their anti-establishment spirit, they usually manage to include a few barbed comments—aimed, for example, at the social pretensions of their hosts:

> *Fashionable Mr. Rai,*
> *Wears a watch on his wrist,*
> *His hair finely combed,*
> *But only three paise jingle in his pocket!*
> song 10

One of the chief ambitions of performing Bauls is to sing on the radio, even though the fees are paltry and the musical policies of the stations reflect commercialism and superficial popular taste at their worst. Apparently the program directors view folk music as a quaint relic of the past that must be offered up in pretty packaging to satisfy the modern public. Thus, a Baul who normally performs only with an ektara is likely to arrive at the studio to find an assortment of staff musicians with flutes, harmoniums, sitars, tablas, and sometimes even violins, to provide the sentimental background accompaniment that will appeal to the popular taste.

A handful of Bauls achieve the status of "superstars," their voices heard regularly on the radio and on public loudspeakers that play the latest recordings. These are the ones whose names spring to the minds of most Bengalis whenever the word "Baul" is mentioned. They are good singers who, because of the commercialization of their art, have had the bite taken out of their lyrics as well as their music.

Though some Bauls make a reasonable living as performers, most are poor, and with the exception of a very few, even the "superstars" cannot be considered rich.

HINDU AND MUSLIM BAULS

*I*n a country where violent hostility often erupts between Muslims and Hindus, Bauls are a unique example of religious integration. They draw their followers from both communities and embrace the essential truths of both faiths while discarding their external, institutionalized aspects.

According to Bauls, there are four subsects among them. However, most Bauls are unclear about the distinctions between the different sects. The Aul and Baul subsects are Hindu-oriented, while the Sain and Darbesh subsects are Muslim-inclined.

At first glance it may be hard to distinguish between a Hindu and a Muslim Baul, for among both groups the men wear colorful robes, scarves, turbans, and beads. There are subtle differences, however. The male Hindu Baul is usually clean-shaven and has long hair tied on top of his head. He often wears a saffron-colored tunic over a similarly colored *dhoti* (a large rectangular piece of fine cotton cloth worn around the waist). His necklace beads are made of *tulasi,* or *tulsi* (holy basil) wood. In contrast, the male Muslim Baul generally has short hair and a trimmed beard, and wears a multicolored *lungi* (a cotton cloth wrapped skirtlike around the lower body) and a loose-fitting patchwork robe. His necklace is normally made of glass, stone, or lotus beads. The women in both communities wear saris. The Hindu women usually wear saffron or white saris, while the Muslim women (of whom there are extremely few) wear saris of many colors.

Muslim Bauls are commonly known as *Fakirs,* meaning itinerant mendicants; or they may be called *Darbeshes,* the Bengali version of the word "dervishes." Muslim Bauls reject the fundamentalism of Islam and its repressive code of law, the Shariat. They seek only the Light that is Allah and His manifested expression, Love, whom they call Navi (a name for the Prophet). To them, Muhammad represents the silent "witness" within. Both Muslim and Hindu Bauls rely for spiritual direction on a guru. The Muslim Bauls call their guru *murshid,* while the Hindus call theirs *gosain.*

One witnesses the social and spiritual integration of the Bauls at the various communal gatherings and festivals. Once I was at a Muslim festival where thousands of chickens were being sacrificed at the mosque. Just out-

◆

side the sacred perimeter was a group of Muslim mendicants, Fakirs, and Bauls. Addressing the pilgrims, one of the Bauls sang Lalan's famous song:

> *On circumcision a man becomes a Muslim;*
> *What rite defines the woman?*
> *A brahmin's sacred cord is his symbol;*
> *How should one recognize his wife?*
>
> > *song 5*

After each verse, the Baul asked the Fakirs to cry out the name of Allah. As a gesture of good faith, they chanted, "Haribol, Haribol" the Bengali chant in praise of Krishna. Many Muslim Bauls were born into the Hindu community but later came under the influence of Sufi teachers. The most famous of such Bauls was Lalan Fakir, who lived in the nineteenth century. As a child he was stricken with smallpox and left for dead by the side of the road. A passing Muslim holy man took the boy home, cured him, and adopted him into his family. Though Lalan did embrace the external aspects of Islam, he was uncompromising in his denunciation of its restrictive practices. Lalan rose to public prominence largely because his songs attracted the attention and admiration of Rabindranath Tagore.

Most Bauls are identified with the Hindu sect known as Vaishnavism. In their songs the Bauls not only borrow religious images directly from Vaishnavism, but also incorporate the poetic forms of its literature.

Interestingly, if one asks non-Baul Vaishnavas whether they consider Bauls to be Vaishnavas, the answer is invariably no; but Bauls—whether of Hindu or Muslim orientation—usually reply with a definite yes. This is probably because the Bauls' definition is a secular one, like that of the original Vaishnavas, who accepted people of all castes and creeds into their fold.

Broadly defined, Vaishnavas are those who worship the god Vishnu, the second member of the Hindu trinity (Brahma the Creator, Vishnu the Preserver, and Shiva the Transcendental). The other two major Hindu cults are the Shaivas, who worship Shiva, and the Shaktas, who are devoted to the goddess Shakti, the universal feminine principle. In classical Indian tradition, there is no distinct cult dedicated to the worship of Brahma.

According to Hinduism, Vishnu periodically incarnates on earth to save the world from chaos and annihilation. Since the beginning of time there have been nine incarnations of Vishnu, in either animal or human form. His tenth incarnation, known as Kalki, is yet to come.

Krishna, the eighth incarnation of Vishnu, is the one whom the Bauls love and worship above all others. Indeed, Vaishnavism in Bengal is synonymous with the cult of Krishna. Many Vaishnavas regard Krishna not merely as a divine incarnation but as the Supreme Deity. The Hindu scriptures offer various accounts of Krishna—as a king, as a heroic warrior, as the charioteer-god of the *Bhagavad Gita,* and as a mischievous child. But it is Krishna as the sensuous and playful adolescent lover that the Bauls revere. In particular, the legends of Krishna's amorous exploits with Radha dominate the imagery of the Bauls' songs and are of great significance to their spiritual path.

The Love-Dalliance of Radha and Krishna

Legends state that Krishna was a cowherder who lived in Vrindaban, beside the river Yamuna (or Jumuna), south of Delhi. As a young man he charmed the *Gopis*—the cowherding village girls and women—with his divine beauty and the enchanting music of his flute. They could not help falling in love with him, and at night they would steal away from their husbands to be in his company. Krishna in turn loved them all so dearly that he musically multiplied his form so that he could dance and make love with all the Gopis at the same time.

Of all the Gopis, Radha was Krishna's favorite. The Radha-Krishna legends describe their love-dalliance in emotional, erotic, and spiritual terms. They appear both as human lovers and as cosmic deities, enacting the divine *Lila,* the eternal play of Creation, in the paradisaical forests of Vrindaban. In these myths, Radha and Krishna are both depicted as adolescents experiencing the joys and mysteries of puberty in all its freshness. Like the youthful Himalayas in spring, the love of Radha and Krishna bursts into a thousand blossoms.

For the Vaishnavas of Bengal, especially the Bauls, the love-dalliance of Radha and Krishna is not just an ancient myth; it is an eternal theme and the very heart of their philosophy. Radha represents the feminine principle at its purest, the insatiable and selfless passion of the devotee for her Beloved. Krishna, the masculine principle, is the experiencer of total bliss and ecstatic love. The sublime delight that Radha and Krishna experience in their union represents the highest state of consciousness.

It is said that in Vrindaban, all beings, with the exception of Krishna, are women—indicating that only passionate and sensuous devotees like Krishna's lovers are able to enter his garden of ecstasy. Thus the Bauls aspire to become like Radha, with the soul yearning passionately for union with Krishna, the Divinity within.

> *Those who become like Gopis*
> *Know the atmosphere*
> *Of Krishna's playground.*
> *Only* they *really know*
> *How to catch the Uncatchable.*
>
> song 32

Bauls use various names of Krishna in their songs to express his playful,

*'Bahurupi', meaning those who dress up as
Radha and Krishna, at a bus stop in Bolpur.
Photo by Bhaskar Bhattacharyya.*

◆

amorous aspect. He is called the Uncatchable Man because his nature is
elusive, inaccessible to the ordinary state of human consciousness. He is
called the Sahaja Man, meaning that his ways are natural and effortless. As
the beloved of his devotees, he is the Man of the Heart. When in his radiant
form he dispels the darkness of ignorance, he is called the Jewel Man or the
Golden Man. He is also the Ferryman who takes one safely across the waters
of Existence. And as the fully realized being who is in constant union with
the Divine, he is known as the Yogi.

Radha is called Viyogini, the maiden separated from her lover and
passionately longing to be with him. As the sensual enchantress who seduces

the Yogi, she is called Yoga Mohini Yogini. She is also the Water Maiden, full of sweet sentiments; and the Flower Girl, full of honey. When in union they become a single inseparable form, Radha-Krishna are called Yugal Kishore, the Youthful United Couple.

The erotic play of Krishna and the Gopis, which might appear illicit and irreligious from a conventional point of view, is sacred and divine in the songs of the Bauls. Not only Hindu Bauls but Muslims, too, sing fervently of Radha and Krishna, often in conjunction with Islamic myths or concepts:

> *If you want to see the Golden Man,*
> *Come closer!*
> *Know the four principles*
> *Of* Nachut, Lahut, Malkut, *and* Jabarut.
>
> song 60

HISTORICAL INFLUENCES

The Bauls' origins are shrouded in mystery, for there is little written evidence of their history and, as itinerants by nature, they have left few tracks. As musicians, it is likely that they are part of an ancient tradition of wandering troubadours, though the songs sung by the Bauls of today are mostly from the nineteenth and twentieth centuries. Much of Baul theology can be traced back to the seventeenth century, whereas Baul sexual-yogic practices have an ancient origin, probably going back to at least the first millennium.

We can guess that the Bauls' present identity developed over a period of several hundred years. Each Baul, when initiated, is told of the number of previous gurus in his or her lineage. The average is about fourteen, and the maximum that I have heard of is eighteen. Taking thirty years as a conservative estimate for each generation, we can thus place the first Baul guru between the mid-fifteenth and-sixteenth centuries, about the time of Chaitanya and other medieval love-mystics. This conclusion seems reasonable, for the Bauls of today are the only surviving ecstatics who embody the revolutionary spirit of the medieval saints of India.

Although we cannot say with exact certainty when the Bauls began to forge their unique identity, we can look into the history of the various religious movements that have influenced their philosophy and way of life. The four major movements that have shaped the Baul way are Tantrism, Vaishnavism, the medieval spiritual reformers, and Sufism. From the Tantrics the Bauls received the heart of their mystical practices; from the Vaishnavas, their theological tenets and lyrical expression; from the medieval reformers, their social liberalism; and from the Sufis, their dance movements, music, and love for *Manush,* or Man.

Tantrism

Tantras are ancient Hindu and Buddhist scriptures dealing with yogic practices, magical rites, metaphysics, and philosophy. Though its antiquity cannot be accurately documented, Tantrism seems to have become well defined by the start of the first millennium A.D. Many Tantrics, however, believe that many of the elements of their practices originated in pre-Aryan times (before 2000 B.C.). Certainly Tantrism has elements in common with the pre-Aryan religion, such as animistic motifs, goddess cults, and sexual yoga; but whether these elements can be placed in the same category as the highly formalized scriptures known as Tantras is a matter of uncertainty. It seems likely that Tantrism has always managed to express itself through the various religious movements with which it has come into contact. When in contact with Buddhism, it expressed itself through Buddhist motifs, and when it came into contact with Vaishnavism, it took on that sect's poetics.

According to the Tantras, caste, sex, and creed do not limit one's capacity for spiritual development. Only through earnest desire, proper knowledge, and diligent effort can the spiritual aspirant advance. This point of view contrasts with that of the Vedas, the authoritative scriptures of orthodox Hinduism. The Vedas emphasize the social and religious order—the relationship between God, humans, and society—whereas the Tantras indicate how the individual can develop a holistic, mystical approach to the Divinity within.

One of the Tantric tenets that is important in the Baul way of life concerns the role of the guru. Though a person may gain an intellectual

Icon of the goddess Kali, garlanded with hibiscus flowers. Photo by Nik Douglas.

knowledge of Tantrism from its scriptures, only a guru can explain the secrets of its yogic practices. This spiritual path has been likened to the sharp edge of a razor, for a slight imbalance can plunge the aspirant into the abysmal depths of degradation, confusion, and suffering. Thus, to attempt the exacting and precarious disciplines leading to spiritual development in the Tantric tradition, one cannot depend merely on written instruction; one must be led by a competent guide, the guru.

In Tantrism the guru is the sole spiritual authority, above all scriptures and testaments; the guru is viewed as the Divinity in human form. Knowledge and love can be lit from another; distinctions disappear when flame touches flame, and similarly there is no real separation between guru and disciple. Ultimately, the guru principle resides within the human self; this is the inner light that dispels the darkness of ignorance and removes all suffering. A Baul song sums up the inner longing:

> O *Guru, pierce my eye*
> *With the needle of discernment*
> *So that I may see the light.*
>
> *song 18*

The role of the guru is prevalent in all Indian religions. But it is only in those sects that have been influenced by Tantrism that the guru principle is viewed not only as masculine but also as feminine. In the Tantric tradition the role of woman is tremendously important, unlike in the Vedic tradition, where she is relegated to a subsidiary position.

The cult of the Goddess is nowhere stronger in India than in Bengal, which is one of the most important centers of Tantrism. There, Shakti, the feminine principle, is worshiped in all her forms: as a virgin, a seductress, a whore, a benevolent mother, and a terrifying destroyer. She is called Kali, the black goddess who consumes *kala,* time. She is also called the Primordial Form, for out of her awesome being the myriad forms of the universe arise, and into her all things merge. Her altars are painted red each morning and red hibiscus flowers are used to garland her image.

The main Bengali festival is the autumnal celebration in honor of Durga, the form of the Goddess as the slayer of demons and the restorer of harmony and peace. During this festival, people from all walks of life—students, farmers, politicians, housewives, children—are swept into the frenzy of her worship. Even Bauls, who are not worshipers of Durga, sing at these celebrations.

The Bauls inherited the concept of the importance of the feminine principle from Tantrism by way of Sahajiya Buddhism and, later, Sahajiya Vaishnavism. It might be more accurate to say that the Bauls adapted the formal conceptualization of Shakti to suit their already existent beliefs. The same may be said for the concept of the guru. In both Tantric and Baul philosophy these two concepts have been integrated. As guru, the woman

initiates the disciple into sexual practices, for it is she who is the "knower" of
the mysterious dynamics of passion and love, she who opens the door to
sensual experience and guides the disciple through the labyrinths of
suprasensory perceptions.

> Someone else has the key to my house.
> How will I get to see its wealth?
> . . .

If the lady at the door is willing,
She will leave it open;
Unable to recognize her,
I wander about in dark alleys.

song 47

At a worldly level, the Bauls share the social outlook of the original Tantrics. They reject the belief that brahmins are the divinely ordained spiritual authority. Unlike Vedic worship, Tantric rites may be performed by everyone. Only an individual's spiritual competency determines the nature of worship that he or she may perform successfully. Whether the Tantric social outlook influenced the Bauls directly or whether they shared the same outlook by coincidence is a matter of conjecture. In any case, the Bauls still hold tenaciously to this viewpoint in both theory and practice, whereas most present-day Tantrics have withdrawn into the folds of brahminism.

Prior to the seventeenth century, Tantrism in Bengal was more intellectual than devotional, and most hymns were in Sanskrit. Subsequently Bengali Tantrism became more emotional and devotional songs appeared in Bengali, the language of the common people. These songs were simple, often ecstatic and poignant, filled with pathos and humility. The singers poured their hearts out to Kali much as the Bauls do to Radha. To convey their visions, these minstrel devotees of Kali used the poetic forms and devotional intensity characteristic of Vaishnavism. The greatest of these minstrels was Ramaprasad, who lived in the eighteenth century. In his mystic trances, he would converse with the Goddess in song—sometimes lamenting his inability to see his beloved Shyama (another name for Kali), the Dark-Hued Girl; at other times exulting at the sight of her beside him. Ramaprasad's songs are still heard throughout Bengal—on the radio, in large temples, in humble homes, and in the charnel grounds. Bauls, too, sing Ramaprasad's songs, especially when they visit shrines dedicated to Kali.

O my heart,
Sing the name of Kali
Over and over again.

. . .

She plays in the charnel grounds,
My beloved Shyama.

. . .

Bhava Pagla, composer of numerous Baul songs and guru to many Bauls. Photo by Georges Luneau.

◆

Look over there on the funeral pyre,
How man's ego burns
Day and night.

A contemporary devotee of Kali whose songs the Bauls also sing is Bhava Pagla, who lives in a small village in the district of Burdwan. A legend in his own time, this extraordinary man is known for his magical presence, his musical virtuosity, and his prolific output of songs. Bhava is said to have composed over forty thousand songs, and there is hardly a Baul who does not know at least one of them.

It would be difficult for any cult in Bengal not to be affected by Tantrism. In every village and town there is a shrine dedicated to Kali and Shiva. The everyday rituals that are observed, such as for births, marriages, funerals, and bathing, are imbued with Tantric overtones. In such an environment, the Bauls, with their highly eclectic tendencies, could not but be influenced by the Tantras.

Vaishnavism

The most significant influence on the Bauls has been that of Vaishnavism. Many divergent groups exist within this sect, but for the Bauls the most important are the Sahajiya Vaishnavas. Sahajiya Vaishnavism is actually a synthesis of two seemingly incompatible cults, the Sahajiyas and the Vaishnavas, that started to integrate around the twelfth century. The orthodox elements in mainstream Vaishnavism today, however, deny that the Sahajiyas are their distant relatives; they view the Sahajiyas as Tantrics in the guise of Vaishnavas.

Sahajiyas are those whose worship is *sahaja,* meaning effortless, natural, or spontaneous. To them, spontaneous human feelings such as lust, anger, and greed were to be understood as qualitative degrees of the same energy that gives rise to positive emotions such as love, generosity, and caring. Rather than reject or repress the destructive emotions, the Sahajiyas sought to harness their power and transform them into a harmonious flow of positive energy. They composed many songs that expressed, in enigmatic symbols, their fundamental concept of the body as microcosm.

The early Sahajiyas were Buddhist Tantrics who practiced sexual-yogic rites. Many of them seem to have been people whose moral and social outlook was at odds with the prevailing social milieu. They flourished under the dynasty of Pala kings who ruled Bengal from the eighth to the twelfth century. The Palas were sympathetic to Buddhist ideals and especially to those doctrines that had Tantric undercurrents.

There are two possible reasons why the Sahajiya cult had its base among the vernacular-speaking common people rather than the Sanskrit-educated brahmins. First, many of the Sahajiya composers of songs probably came from uneducated backgrounds and were not sufficiently versed in Sanskrit. Second, the Buddhists were appealing to the masses, having given up hope of penetrating the narrow brahmin mind. By composing their songs in the vernacular, the Sahajiya poets made their teachings accessible to the common people.

From a study of their songs it appears that, like the Bauls of today, the

Sahajiyas were averse to pedantry, hierarchical authority, scriptural injunctions, and ritualistic piety, seeking instead the joys of the world and the ecstasy of transcendental experience. They rebelled as much against orthodox Buddhism as against Brahminism.

> *Those who go on reciting and explaining*
> *Cannot know the truth.*
> *It is not only unknown*
> *But also unknowable to them.*
>
> *Those who do not drink eagerly (to their heart's*
>   *content)*
> *The nectar of the Guru's instruction*
> *Die of thirst*
> *Like fools deceived by the mirage of the desert.*
>
> *Scholars explain the scriptures,*
> *But do not know of the Buddha*
> *Who resides in their own body;*
> *By such scholarship they can never escape*
> *The cycle of comings and goings.*
> *Yet those shameless creatures think themselves to*
>   *be Pundits.* *

Sahajiya Vaishnavism

At the beginning of the twelfth century, the Buddhist Pala dynasty was replaced by the Senas, who were ardent Vaishnavas. It was during the period of their rule that the theology and poetry of the Sahajiyas took on a Vaishnava rather than a Buddhist tone, though their mystical practices remained the same. Whether the conversion was motivated by an actual change of heart or was simply a concession to the new rulers, we cannot say. In any case, the shift of emphasis to Vaishnavism gave the Sahajiyas a warmer, more emotional appeal.

---

* Saraha in Doha-Kosa, composed around the tenth century. Quoted in S. B. Dasgupta, *Obscure Religious Cults*, p. 61.

For all its colorful imagery, the Sahajiya doctrine was cold and speculative, as much of Tantric doctrine had become. Such an approach may satisfy the intellectually inclined, but the hard-working, uneducated peasants responded more to the emotional expression offered by Vaishnava mythology—in particular the Krishna theme, for here was a divine figure, a supreme deity, who nonetheless expressed the full range of human emotions. But even more than Krishna, it was his lovers, the Gopis, who expressed the diversity of moods and sentiments. The Gopis lost themselves in passionate abandon, caring nothing for their own welfare, seeking only the object of their love, and it was they who were idealized by the ecstatic poets.

The Erotic Literature of Vaishnavism

Before the twelfth century there already existed in Bengal a literature that celebrated the love-dalliance of Krishna and the Gopis. This was contained in the basic text of Bengali Vaishnavism, the *Shrimad Bhagavatam* (or *Bhagavata Purana*). However, this text makes no mention of Radha. It is likely that Radha existed as a folk heroine-goddess before the advent of the Sena dynasty, though she was rarely mentioned in Sanskrit religious texts. Secular Sanskrit sources indicate that the popular worship of Radha-Krishna was already common. The Sanskrit poet Dimbocka wrote in the twelfth century that "the city folk are waked at dawn by pilgrims in the street. With patchwork cloaks sewn of a hundred rags, they ward off the winter cold. Their voices are pure and clear as they sing of the holy lore of Krishna and Radha."*

Jayadeva's *Gita Govinda*

Radha appeared in popular Sanskrit literature for the first time in the celebrated lyrical drama *Gita Govinda* ("Song of the Cowherd") by the twelfth-century mystic and poet Jayadeva. This beautiful work, noted for its sensual eroticism and delicate poetic expression, still remains a unique source of inspiration. In it, Radha is exalted to so high a status that she herself becomes an object of worship equal to Krishna. Whether or not this was due to the inherent Bengali tendency to extol the feminine principle remains an interesting question. The *Gita Govinda* conveys the extremes of emotion

---

*From Daniel H. Ingalls, *A Sanskrit Poetry of Village and Field: Yogeswara and His Fellow Poets.*

experienced by Radha and Krishna from the first moment of their infatuation, through the anguish of separation, to the final ecstasy of union.

Separated from Krishna, Radha laments, deep in anguish.

> *Has he waylaid some loving girl?*
> *Do his friends hold him by clever tricks?*
> *Is he roaming blindly near the dark forest?*
> *Or does my lover's anguished mind so tangle*
> *   the path*
> *That he cannot come into this thicket of vines*
> *And sweet swamp reeds where we promised*
> *   to meet?*
>
> **Gita Govinda 7.11**

> *Sandalwood mountain wind,*
> *As you blow southern breezes*
> *To spread the bliss of love,*
> *Soothe me! End the paradox!*
> *Lifebreath of the world,*
> *If you bring me Madhava*
> *For a moment*
> *You may take my life!*
>
> **Gita Govinda 7.39**

Later, Krishna returns and proclaims his passion.

> *Let pearls quivering on full breasts*
> *Move the depths of your heart!*
> *Let a girdle ringing on round hips*
> *Proclaim the command of Love!*
> *Radha, cherished love,*
> *Abandon your baseless pride!*
> *Love's fire burns my heart—*
> *Bring wine in your lotus mouth!*
>
> **Gita Govinda 10.6 ***

---

* Translation by Barbara Stoller Miller, *Love Song of the Dark Lord: Jayadeva's Gita Govinda* (New York: University of Columbia Press, 1977).

Such was the popularity of the *Gita Govinda* that it was sung in temples, at religious fairs, and in royal courts. Scholars recited it and minstrels sang it. By virtue of its divine aspirations, the work's open sensuality was accepted, even though during this period sexuality was considered unmentionable in public.

Jayadeva became recognized as a saint. To this day, hundreds of Bauls hold their most important festival at mid-January each year in the Bengali village of Kenduli, where, according to legend, Jayadeva lived with his beloved wife Padmavati. The Sahajiyas claim that Jayadeva was one of them, but the more traditional Vaishnavas refute their claim by pointing out the lack of apparent Sahajiya doctrine in the *Gita Govinda*. Does it matter? Surely it is a measure of Jayadeva's greatness that he was, and is still, a source of inspiration for people of diverse natures.

Chandidas

The other mystic poet who has had considerable influence upon the Bauls is Badu Chandidas. Indeed, he has greatly affected the social, devotional, and philosophical attitudes of the Bengalis. Even today, at religious festivals and gatherings, his poems, called *Ragatmika-Pada* ("Songs of Passionate Devotion"), are sung and recited by Vaishnavas and non-Vaishnavas alike. His appeal is immediate and uncomplicated, for even though his songs express higher aspirations and gratifications through Hindu motifs, their spirit is universal. It is this universality that has made him one of the best loved of Bengali visionary poets.

Among scholars there is much controversy surrounding Chandidas. The earliest known date for Chandidas's songs is around the mid-fourteenth century and the latest around the mid-fifteenth. Though well over two thousand songs have been attributed to him, some are obviously by lesser-known Sahajiya poets of the seventeenth and eighteenth centuries. Since many of these songs are critical of the established order and are overtly sexual in content, it may be that some poets used the name Chandidas as a convenient pseudonym in order to avoid social abuse and scorn.

According to one legend, Chandidas was a Tantric who lived in Nanur in the Birbhum district. He was a worshiper of Vasuli, a Sahajiya form of the goddess Durga, the tutelary deity of his family village. However, like many other Bengali poets, though he belonged to a particular religious sect,

Chandidas often used the religious motifs of other sects in his verses. In the collection of poems known as *Srikrishna-kirtan*, Chandidas sings of Radha's love for Krishna.

> *Tell me,*
> *Tell me, my beautiful love,*
> *Why do your limbs appear numb,*
> *Lips tremble*
> *And eyes well up with tears?*
>
> *Shivers surrounding your delicate frame*
> *Choke your life*
> *As you silently brood,*
> *Gazing at nothing.*
> *What do you think and what do you see?*
>
> *Says Badu Chandidas:*
> *I know for sure,*
> *The flute has entered her ears.**

The faintest traces of Sahajiya doctrine in these poems are not sufficient proof that Chandidas was a Sahajiya. However, as a Tantric who worshiped Vasuli and was inspired by the Radha-Krishna theme, he may at least be considered sympathetic to the Sahajiyas.

On the other hand, the poets who composed the verses attributed to Chandidas probably were practicing Sahajiyas. Their songs are of greater importance to the Bauls.

> *Find your match*
> *In a worthy love*
> *Before you lose your heart.*
> *Love is a jewel*
> *To be guarded with care*

---

* This and the following extract are from Deben Bhattacharyya, *Love Songs of Chandidas* (London: George Allen and Unwin, 1967).

When lovers are equal
In maturity.

According to another legend, Chandidas was a brahmin who committed the ultimate sacrilege of falling in love with a low-caste washerwoman named Rajakini. Despite the urgent pleas of his family not to indulge in such folly, he plunged deeper into the relationship. Such was the couple's devotion that all the scorn and ridicule of the community only strengthened their love. For Chandidas, Rajakini was an incarnation of Radha, and it was to her that he made obeisance.

Like Jayadeva, Chandidas believed that Radha was to be worshiped with the same intensity as Krishna; that in no way was her role in the divine Lila any less than his. Indeed, without her bliss-giving power, Krishna is unable to enact his cosmic play. But whereas Jayadeva wrote the *Gita Govinda* in Sanskrit, Chandidas wrote his songs in Bengali, the language of the common people. This made his songs popular with people from all walks of life.

There were other poets of the twelfth to fifteenth centuries, not necessarily Vaishnavas or Sahajiyas, who influenced the Bauls, but many of their names are unknown; written records either were never made or were lost in floods or hurricanes. One poet who is well known was a non-Bengali named Vidyapati (1368–1476). His songs, devoted to the amorous adventures of Radha and Krishna, were in the same emotional vein as Jayadeva's and Chandidas's.

The Medieval Spiritual Reformers

The social and religious atmosphere in India during the fifteenth and sixteenth centuries was oppressive and restrictive, especially so in Bengal. A strong and autocratic Muslim rule held sway over northern India. Hindu temples were pulled down and desecrated, and devout Hindus were tyrannized by some of the less enlightened Muslim rulers, who looked down on the Hindus as lazy dreamers and superstitious idol worshipers. The Hindus in turn saw Muslims as coarse, unclean, and violent in their religious ideals. Mutual disrespect, social animosity, and religious intolerance prevailed.

If the tyranny outside Hinduism was oppressive, so was the tyranny within. The orthodox brahmins, held to be the sole religious authority by divine right, determined the moral and ethical code of Hindu society. With their extremely conservative social outlook, they created and codified a social-religious system whose inflexibility prevented any form of creative evolution. Fearing the infiltration of Muslim ideology, the Hindus withdrew deeper into the confines of the caste system. The ancient laws governing this system were made more rigid and the barriers to social intercourse between the castes were strengthened. Large numbers of low-caste Hindus converted to Islam to win the favor of the rulers and gain greater economic freedom.

In Bengal, the prudery of brahminism existed alongside the irresponsibility and licentiousness of those who called themselves Tantrics. Without understanding the disciplines of Tantrism, these people embraced its more erotic and outrageous tenets, such as the rite of the five sacraments (fish, meat, grain, alcohol, and sexual intercourse), and often abused them. Some of these people came from criminal backgrounds; by putting on religious robes, they were able to sanctify their vices in the eyes of society. Such self-styled "holy" men and women tyrannized the Bengali rural folk, playing on their superstitious fears and threatening them with magical retribution if they did not pay subservient homage.

It was during this dark age of Indian history that there arose in the North various individuals and movements that sought to reform not only the prevalent religious attitudes but the social conditions as well. Characterized by social liberalism and emotional religious fervor, these movements embraced a nonintellectual, nonritualistic approach to spirituality. Many of the prominent figures of this period were noted poets as well as reformers.

Kabir

One of the best-loved Indian poets, Kabir (1440–1518) was a poor Muslim weaver who lived in Benares (also known as Kashi), the center of orthodox Hinduism. Kabir had the moral courage to speak out against the hypocrisy and depravity of those who purported to be the bastions of religious order. Though Kabir was an iconoclast, he was also deeply spiritual, and it was this mixture of irreverence and natural piety that made him popular. Influenced by both the Sufis and the Sahajiya Vaishnavas, he took up their love-mysticism and championed the cause of Hindu-Muslim unity.

> *The Hindu died crying "Ram!"*
> *The Mussulman crying "Khuda!"*

Kabir, that one will live
Who keeps away from both!

Now the Kaaba has become Kashi,
Ram has become Rahim;
Coarse meal has become fine flour,
And Kabir sits down to enjoy it! *

Kabir's mysticism was an uncompromising spiritual quest, with yoga as its base, echoing the concept of "truth within the body."

O ignorant one,
That Yogi, my Guru, will sing this song.
There stands a tree without any roots:
It bears fruit but no blossoms.
Without branches or leaves,
It raises its head to the eight heavens.
Leaves without root, arms without a body,
It sings songs without a tongue.
The Guru will make it clear that
The singer has no form. Kabir says:
It is hard to find the path
Of the fish and the kite.
I am a sacrifice to that Being
Whose compassion is boundless.[†]

As this poem demonstrates, Kabir's verse is close in spirit to the songs of the Bauls. Kabir integrated that aspect common to all true spirituality, the transcendental power of love.

Kabir, on that steed of Love
With full consciousness, I mounted:
Taking in hand the sword of wisdom,
I struck Death a great blow on the head![††]

---

* From Charlotte Vaudeville, *Kabir* (New York: Oxford University Press, 1974). Ram is the seventh incarnation of Vishnu. Khuda and Rahim are Arabic terms for God.

† Free translation by Bhaskar Bhattacharyya.

†† Vaudeville, op. cit.

Guru Nanak

Guru Nanak (1438–1568), born a Hindu in the Punjab in northwestern India, sought to unite Hinduism and Islam and became the founder of Sikhism. Nanak wandered with the Vaishnavas, Sufis, and Tantrics. He too believed in a casteless society that would respect all forms of religion.

It is said that once, while spending the night in a mosque on his way to Mecca, Nanak fell asleep with his feet toward the sacred Kaaba. The mullah of the mosque was incensed by this, for it was equivalent to turning the feet toward God, an act of great disrespect. The mullah woke Nanak and reproached him angrily. Nanak retorted: "Turn my feet in a direction where there is neither God nor the Kaaba."

For Nanak, God was formless, beyond description. To realize this absolute Reality, the seeker must tread the path of righteousness, with the guru as his guide.

Guru Nanak's songs are compiled in an anthology called the *Adi Granth*. The first morning prayer, called "Japji," sung by the Sikhs, bears the essence of Nanak's message:

> *There is One God*
> *His Name is Truth*
> *He is the Creator*
> *He is without fear and without hate*
> *Beyond time, immortal,*
> *His spirit pervades the universe.*
> *Neither is He born*
> *Nor does He die to be born again,*
> *For He is self-existent.*
> *You shall worship Him*
> *With the Guru's grace.*

Mirabai

In Vrindaban, the "playground" of Krishna, the beautiful Mira (1498–1540), or Mirabai, enchanted people with her love songs dedicated to her beloved Krishna. Mira was a princess who had renounced power and glory in favor of a simple spiritual life devoted to her Lord. Whether Mirabai was a practicing Sahajiya is difficult to ascertain, but her passionate longing for Krishna displayed all the sentiments of a truly devoted lover.

> *The separated sleepless,*
>   *When the world sleeps, friend,*
>
> *One strings pearls in her palace*
>   *Another threads tears,*
> *The night has passed,*
>   *Counting the stars,*
> *Mira waits for the Hour-of-Pleasure*
>   *When the Dark-One will*
>   *Take away her pain.* *

Like the Bauls, Mirabai worshiped directly from the heart, without outer rituals or observances.

> *Sheltered, sheltered,*
> *The Eternal*
> *My shelter,*
>
> *Not japa and tapa,†*
> *Not mantra and tantra,*
> *Not in Kashi*
> *Not in the Vedas,*
> *Mira's Lord is Ghirdhara,*
> *She bows before his Lotus-feet.*

Mirabai's songs of praise, known as *Mira-bhajans,* are still sung throughout India. Originally composed in Brajbhasa, the Hindi dialect of the Vrindaban region, they have been converted into Bengali versions by the Bauls, who acknowledge Mira as one of their saints.

Dadu

Dadu (1544–1603), a Muslim cotton-carder born in Gujarat in western India, renounced the world as a young man, and wandered and preached in

---

* This and the following extracts are translated by Louise Landes-Levi, from an unpublished manuscript.

† *Japa* is the recitation of a mantra, and *tapa* are penances.

and around Rajasthan. Though he had been initiated by a Sufi master, Dadu's personal deity was Rama, the seventh incarnation of Vishnu. Like Kabir, whom he revered, Dadu believed in the "God within" and had little patience with external religion. Of the brahmins he said:

> They are called the sons of Brahman,
> But their minds are devoid of discernment.
> They expound their sacred scriptures,
> While evil spirits dance within. *

Dadu was no less critical of the Muslims:

> The tiger, the lion, the jackal and all the rest—
> How many Musalmans there are!
> By eating flesh, they become "believers":
> Such is the wisdom of their pious instructor.
> They cut throats and recite the creed:
> Such is their miserable cult.
> They say prayers five times a day,
> But honest conviction have they none.

Despite the acerbic tone of his songs, Dadu was a truly spiritual man. He deeply impressed Akbar, the most enlightened of the Mogul emperors, who was dissatisfied with orthodox Islam and often invited teachers of various religions to his court for discussions.

Dadu's doctrines were embodied in the *Bani*, a collection of sayings, verses, and songs:

> *(Refrain)*
> He is Light, Light, from first to last:
> Eternal, changeless, filling all creation.
>
> 1. In the heavens, Light, on the earth, Light:
>   the Holy Provider;
>   In the water, Light, in the air, Light:
>   the source of all excellencies.

---

* The three passages from Dadu quoted here are from W. G. Orr, *A Sixteenth-Century Indian Mystic* (London: Lutterworth Press, 1947).

2. Without and within, present and beholding all,
   art Thou, the wise Ruler.
   I have beheld the strange and marvellous Light:
   Dadu is overwhelmed.

Chaitanya

It would be difficult to imagine Bengali life without the influence of Chaitanya (1485–1534), known to his followers as Mahaprabhu, "Great Master." He revived the spirit of Vaishnavism and gave it a seductive and appealing form. To Bauls, Sri Chaitanya is the single most important figure in their history. Many Vaishnava Bauls consider Chaitanya to be the original Baul.

Chaitanya was born a brahmin in the Navadip area of Bengal. As a schoolboy he displayed a prodigious intellect; legend has it that he mastered the main branches of Sanskrit learning by the age of fifteen. After his father died, the responsibility of supporting the family fell to the still-young Chaitanya. He married and soon established his own school, where he received many students.

As an intellectual, Chaitanya showed no interest in religion and often mocked those who tried to convert him. But at the age of twenty-two he underwent a sudden transformation. He had gone to the pilgrimage town of Gaya in Bihar to perform holy rites in memory of his father. It was there that, after receiving initiation from his guru, Isvara Puri, he was overwhelmed by an intense spiritual experience. His interest in intellectual and scholastic pursuits having disappeared, Chaitanya lost himself in blissful visions of Krishna. He returned to Navadip raving like a madman, singing Krishna's name without cease. Neglecting his personal appearance, he danced in the streets, laughing and weeping with abandon, heedless of social convention.

As Chaitanya's spiritual vision became more and more consuming, his sense of the world faded away. Obviously he could no longer continue his profession as a teacher, and the financial situation at home deteriorated. Anxious and bewildered, his family and friends were powerless to do any-thing about the situation. But a small group of local Vaishnavas saw through the facade of lunacy and recognized Chaitanya's sublime spiritual status. They regarded him as an embodiment of the dual incarnation of Radha-Krishna: Outwardly, he was Radha, the yearning lover and devotee, while inwardly he was Krishna, the divine object of love and devotion. Whereas the earlier Vaishnava poets, such as Jayadeva and Chandidas, expressed the desire to witness the cosmic love-play of Radha and Krishna, Chaitanya desired to experience their ecstasy directly.

In the years that followed, Chaitanya drew an enthusiastic following from all walks of life. In his blissful presence, scholars lost their skepticism. On hearing him chant Krishna's name, peasants felt their burdens lifted. Children relished seeing him play like one of them, and lovers wept on hearing his poignant laments. The doctrine of devotion, or *Bhakti*, which Chaitanya practiced and preached, appealed to the Bengali people for its simplicity and directness. On the path of Bhakti, there are no religious, economic, or social distinctions: Only by the power of devotion can one reach the eternal abode of Krishna. Chaitanya taught that the devotee must become like Radha and love Krishna with passionate fervor. He must give up selfishness and perform all duties and services for Krishna alone.

According to Chaitanya, Bhakti could best be expressed by continuously chanting Krishna's name. He and his followers would gather together every evening in a courtyard and devote themselves to the form of worship known as *sankirtan* (or *kirtan*)—chanting and singing and dancing to the accompaniment of cymbals, bells, and drums. As the night wore on, the singing would become more energetic, the rhythms would beat faster, the dancing would become less restrained, and all were carried away in the abandon of ecstasy. This highly emotional atmosphere often gave rise to mystical trances.

Often Chaitanya and his followers would take to the streets, singing and dancing in procession, spreading the message of Bhakti with such passion that people's hearts were irresistibly moved. It was this kind of powerful expression that was the force behind the movement's growth.

Chaitanya left no written teachings, and the accounts of his life and sermons were recorded only by his intimate disciples. Since the various accounts often differed depending on the individual writer's inclinations, many different sects arose after Chaitanya's death, each claiming to represent the authentic tradition of his teaching.

Some sects worshiped Chaitanya as a deity with brahmanical rituals. The Sahajiyas took him to be one of them, believing that hidden behind the apparent simplicity of his message lay mystical practices like their own. Just as the orthodox condemned the Sahajiyas' brazen sexual interpretations of Chaitanya's teachings, so the Sahajiyas in turn ridiculed their puritanical, caste-oriented revisionism. Despite Chaitanya's belief in the equality of all castes, the educated higher castes eventually established their authority over the organized Chaitanya sects, thereby ensuring that the orthodox elements would prevail.

The Bauls and the Sahajiyas chose not to follow any particular school of thought but, like the proverbial bee, drew nectar from various flowers of wisdom.

The following extracts from a contemporary Baul song illustrate how Chaitanya's influence is still alive today:

> *Here comes Chaitanya's train*
> *To Golden Nadia.*
> *Radha's company has assembled*
> *In the courtyard of Srivasa*
>
> *song 27*

> *Don't beat woman, O brother.*
> *When you beat her, you beat the Guru!*
> *The sage Chaitanya has spoken*
> *Of her bashful nature.*
> *Go, place your head at her feet.*
>
> *song 39*

Sufism

While the Bauls received their Hindu influences from the Vaishnavas and Tantrics (who also contributed Buddhist elements), their Muslim influence came from the Sufis. Sufism is an anti-establishment mystical wing considered heretical from the viewpoint of orthodox Islam. Their aim being mystical union with God, the Sufis place greater emphasis on spiritual experience than on scriptural dogma and observances. The Sufi movement flourished in the Arab countries and in Persia, and produced a magnificent literary tradition that expressed the yearning of the lover (the spiritual aspirant) for the Beloved (God), often in ecstatic erotic imagery.

Sufism probably reached Bengal early in the thirteenth century, during the time of the first Muslim invasions. Over the centuries, the Sufi influence spread to those religious-minded people who found it difficult to live with either the despotic social rule of the brahmins or the dogmatic dictates of the Muslim mullahs.

The Sufis' way appealed especially to the poor and downtrodden of India, such as the mendicants, who had for generations been denied religious expression. The Hindu scriptures sanctioned begging as a noble way of life, but only for higher-caste Hindus who had renounced material possessions as a religious act. Those who were born and lived on the streets could only sing the name of God in the hope that some passer-by would toss them a few coins. Sufism gave many of these people a religious authority by which they were granted greater respect.

These Sufis, who became known as Fakirs, took to yoga, sorcery, music, literature, and art. Some were invited to live in palaces and grace the courts of kings with their music and verse. Others remained wandering mendicants. Many fakirs took to extreme practices, performing mortification of the body such as lying on beds of nails. Some were rogues who exploited and intimidated the rural Bengalis.

But it was the love-mysticism of the Sufis that attracted the Bauls, and the rich symbolism of their poetry that inspired them. Among the greatest of the Persian Sufi poets was Jalaluddin Rumi (1207–1273), who taught that God is hidden within man, and the spirit within the flesh, just as the bird is confined within the cage:

> We have become drunk and our heart has departed, it has fled from us —whither has it gone?
>
> When it saw that the chain of reason was broken, immediately my heart took to flight.
>
> It will not have gone to any other place, it has departed to the seclusion of God.
>
> Seek it not in the house, for it is of the air; it is a bird of the air, and has gone into the air.
>
> It is the white falcon of the Emperor; it has taken flight, and departed to the Emperor.*

The image of the bird is used extensively in Baul songs. The Bauls had no difficulty integrating this symbol with their concept of "truth within the body."

---

* A. J. Arberry, *Mystical Poems of Rumi* (Chicago: University of Chicago Press, 1968), no. 89, p. 77.

A Muslim Baul at the great annual festival at Shantiniketan, West Bengal. Photo by Nik Douglas.

◆

The bird sits inside a cage.
It has nine doors.
Through which door does she fly
Both in and out,
Leaving me so confused?

Like the Vaishnavas, the Sufis celebrated the theme of divine love in a story of an amorous couple: the famous tale of Laila and Majnun, of which perhaps the greatest version was written by Nizami Ganjai (1141–1205). Set against the background of tribal warfare in the Arabian desert, it is the story of two lovers defying social convention. Majnun, a rich Arab boy, is in love with Laila, a poor Bedouin girl. Whereas in the Hindu theme, it is woman, as Radha, who represents the yearning lover, here, as Laila, woman is the object of love. In the Sufi tradition, the yearning spirit is said to ascend through seven stages of love, beginning with passionate longing and culminating in ecstatic union, in which there is no distinction between lover, beloved, and love itself.

Among the most important Sufi spiritual practices which the Bauls incorporated into their tradition are the chanting of God's name and His praises, known as *sama,* and the practice of *dhikr,* or remembrance (of God), often accompanied by intoxicating whirling ritual dances. From their Vaishnava heritage, the Bauls were already familiar with communal religious chanting, and because of their own musical tradition they were aware of the power of song and dance in mystical spirituality. It seems likely that the Bauls' whirling dances and musical compositions, especially the melodies, came directly from the Sufi tradition. This is generally true as well of much classical and folk traditions of dance and music of North India as well.

Another feature shared by both the Bauls and the Sufis is the belief in the guru as the sole spiritual authority. The Sufis put greater trust in their guru than in the Shariat or even the Koran itself. Like the Bauls, the Sufis do not discard traditional legends and scriptural themes but use them to illustrate their own beliefs.

It is doubtful whether the Bauls inherited any totally original metaphysics from the Sufis, as they did from the Tantrics and the Vaishnavas; but they did capture the Sufis' uncompromising spirit of freedom and their love for humanity, which is reflected in the concept of *Maner Manush,* the Man of the Heart. Certainly the Bauls also resemble their fellow "madmen" of Afghanistan, Iran, and other Middle Eastern countries, with their patchwork robes, lutelike instruments, and riddle-bound songs.

BAUL COMMUNITIES

Despite their public image, not all Bauls are performing musicians. Among the Bauls I have met, those who are actively engaged in spiritual disciplines never perform publicly. And many Bauls do not sing at all. Nor are all Bauls practicing mystics. Many lead quiet, simple lives, some engaged in farming and everyday household chores, others wandering from one village to another, living off charity.

Though the Bauls' customs may differ greatly from those of the villagers among whom they live, there is nearly always a strong communal bond between both groups. Bauls generally do not keep themselves apart from the villagers. They live in compounds called *akharas* (literally "forts") either within or near a village. An akhara usually consists of several huts, along with mounds that are the graves, or *samadhis*, of the Baul gurus. Often the Bauls use the same pond as the villagers for bathing, laundering, and other household tasks.

Villagers are welcomed at the annual gatherings called *Mahatsabs* ("Great Feasts") at which Bauls commemorate the burial day of the original guru who founded their akhara. In India, though the passing of a guru may be mourned, at the same time his liberation from the bondage of bodily existence is regarded as cause for celebration. A Mahatsab may go on for days, with the akhara looking like a Gypsy encampment. There is continuous music during cooking and eating, at sunset and evening, and, at night, long musical charades. At dawn, the singing becomes a kind of chanting accompanied by small brass cymbals. Mahatsabs are great occasions when both famous and unknown Bauls come together, though the festivals are not exclusively for Bauls. Many local people are invited and often participate actively in the organizational details. People come from nearby villages and beggars from afar. It is at these feasts that one hears the best Baul music. Most of the people are familiar with Baul symbols and philosophy. The powerful melodies and rhythms awaken and excite the Bauls and their audience. The long sustained tremolos pierce the emotions, and the hollow sounds of the goba (the hand drum) echo through the senses. When erotic sentiments are evoked at these gatherings, they become a divine experience. Many people—children and adults—decide to become Bauls on these occasions.

Bauls often play an important part in the life of the community in times of sorrow. A dramatic example of this took place during the monsoon in 1978 in the Birbhum district. It had been drizzling lightly, and I was among a large group of Bauls and villagers who had taken shelter in the cowpen, the only hut large enough to accommodate all of us. Soon the music began, the youngsters singing first, while the elders smoked ganja to heighten their mood.

A family of Bauls at the akhara. Photo
by Bhaskar Bhattacharyya.

◆

After a while the rain became heavier, and in no time a storm was in
full force. Roofs were torn from huts, and goats and cows tore free from
their tethers in fright. In the distance we could hear the violent gushing of
water as the rivers overflowed their banks. The floods had come.

Children were screaming, and adults, too, began to panic. Villagers from
outlying areas began to arrive with horrific accounts of people being swept
away by the torrents, even of entire villages being washed away. Nevertheless, the Bauls continued to sing. In their songs they even teased the villagers
for their despair—though the homes of the Bauls themselves were also in
danger.

Suddenly an elderly woman rushed into the hut, crying that her house
had been destroyed. She pleaded hysterically with the elder Bauls, as gurus,
to relieve her anguish. They merely mumbled a few words and continued

smoking their ganja. The woman persisted in her raving until finally one of the Bauls sharply commanded her to hold her tongue. "Can't you see that we are enjoying ourselves?" he said. "It's true that we've lost everything—but let's worry about that tomorrow when the rains have stopped." Silenced, the old woman withdrew into a corner.

But the rain did not stop the next day. It poured continuously for three days—and all the while, the Bauls went on singing. In time the old woman emerged from her gloom and started to enjoy herself, and the others also calmed down. Despite all the suffering, the devotional fervor of the Bauls' ceaseless singing had lifted their spirits and revived their sense of hope.

> *What wick is in this lamp*
> *That burns in the City*
> *Both night and day?*
> *It burns in the center of the lamp.*
> *See it, O beloved ones!*
> *No winds or rain will make it flicker.*
> *song 58*

Part Two

◆

SONGS OF LOVE AND ECSTASY

The Way of the Bauls

What is the Way of the Bauls?
What sort of Life do they lead?
What are the sexual organs?
From where do they issue?

The Baul worships that
Which is the cause of existence.
Bauls say:
"Life is the Supreme Test."

Life is the Shrine,
The Journey and the Way.
The wandering Baul is the Original One,
Which only few become.

They do not indulge
In metaphysical speculation
Or strive for liberation.
Duddu says:
"Life is the Supreme Test."

Song of Duddu

Everyone Is Mad

Mad, mad...everyone is mad.
Why then rebuke the mad?
With an open mind, see within.
See if anyone is without madness.

Some are mad for riches,
Some about themselves,
Some because they haven't enough;
Some for the form,
Some for the taste;
Some are mad in Love.
Some just cry and laugh
Madness has many forms.

Everyone says, "mad, mad."
Is it the fruit of a tree?

I Have Lost My Mind

I have lost my mind.
I don't know
In what it is lost,
Or why it is in such Bliss.

There is no use
Hiding my madness anymore;
I have lost all sense
Of time and space.
In Bliss this mind dances;
Its bells ring night and day.

Magical is this incredible state.
Where is the sea?
Where is the river?
If you want to know
This Wave of Bliss,
Unite the eye with the heart.

If you want to see
So many colors, O mind,
See with the heart's eye.

4

The Ocean of Love

What fear of death is there
For those who swim
In the Ocean of Love?
Caste, fear, and shame
Are all forever lost.

They do no work
That has no Love.
All orthodox rules of conduct
Are left behind.

They only acknowledge the way
Of the Sensual King of Emotions.
Their religious duties
Are washed away!

Though like madmen, they are not mad.
Two streams flow inward
From their eyes.
Like tributaries of the river Ganges,
They flow and mix within.

Says poor Gopal:
"My own Forgetful One
Is Love-mad,
Floating on the River
Of Divine Emotion."

Song of Gopal

Commentary

For those who are truly in love, there are no obstacles. Love, whether it is for another human soul or for an ideal, supersedes man-made social and moral orders. Krishna, the Sensual King of Emotions, loved Radha, who was the wife of another man, but because of the divine nature of their love, ordinary moral values vanished into insignificance. When lovers unite, they become inseparable, like the tributaries of a river when they join at a confluence.

No Differences

Everyone asks:
"To which caste does Lalan belong?"
Says Lalan:
"I haven't seen any differences."

On circumcision a man becomes a Muslim;
What rite defines the woman?
A brahmin's sacred cord is his symbol;
How should one recognize his wife?

Some people have prayer beads of tulasi.
Others have ones of glass.
Is that what distinguishes religions?
Are there any special signs of caste
At birth or death?

Water is called well water
When it comes out of a hole.
It is known as Ganga water
When it flows in the Ganges.
At Source all water is identical;
Its nature changes
According to the vessel.

Caste distinctions limit the world
Yet people constantly extoll them.
Lalan has argued with such talks
In marketplaces everywhere.

Song of Lalan

6

The Renunciate

One does not become a renunciate
Simply by wearing beads
Or painting the forehead.
What good does it do
To stop eating meat
And become a vegetarian?

Renunciation is not cheap,
To be bought by the sackload.
Otherwise any thief could steal it
And mutter, "Krishna, Krishna."
As a renunciate,
For the rest of your life
You will have to beg to eat!

If you want to embrace renunciation,
In the vessel of devotion
On the fire of faith,
Transform the Essence of Love.

If there are mental afflictions,
You will have to become
Like a plowman's ox.
For the rest of your life
You will have to beg to eat!

Mad Binda suffers such pain,
Unable to find the Man of the Heart.
People who have heard His name,
Have Him to share all troubles.

Song of Binda Khepa

Commentary

Many people in India become renunciates, not out of a genuine yearning for a life of simplicity and detachment or for self-knowledge, but as an escape from the problems of worldly life. A true renunciate is one who has cast aside the ego. Like the work of an ox, getting rid of the ego is a long and strenuous process.

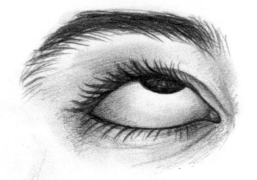

Fix Your Gaze

Fix your gaze with both eyes,
For you are sure to see It
This very lifetime.
There is no deception.
This path we travel on,
The renunciate's path,
Should be knowingly renounced.

First give up the idea
Of reciting mantras.
Know also
That thousands of "mad ones"
Smoking ganja endlessly
Do not get anywhere!

Hindus bicker;
Moslems are deceitful.
Says Duddu:
"I have left all this,
Knowing full well!"

Song of Duddu

There Will Be No Honey Unless You Make It

What good is it being a Baul outside
If there is no honey within?
O mad heart!
There will be no honey unless you make it
For the bee to taste.

Inside the gold, there is copper.
If you go to the goldsmith,
You will surely get caught!
O crazy mind,
Those who go without the real thing
Are known as frauds.

What good is it being beautiful
If, without knowing the rasa within,
You remain unsensuous?
Dancing and prancing, you will wither away;
The sadhaka will have contempt for you.

It's no good just dressing up like a Baul;
No one will mistake tinsel for gold.
Tinsel will never sell at the price of gold!
So says Guru Chand,
Seeing Radha Shyam's stupidity.

Song of Radha Shyam

Everything Is Under Control

Who knows what our karma holds;
The bazaar has been controlled.
Oil is under control,
Sugar is under control,
The government has controlled humans as well!

Meat is ten rupees a kilo.
Fish is almost twelve,
Grains are not less than six.
Seeing eggs at eighty paise a pair,
The brahmin has started to keep poultry!

We live in an independent country
Eating controlled food.
Some have motorcycles between their legs
And others, bamboos up their arses.
Some travel in large cars,
Others go on bamboo stretchers.
With sadness Hara says:
"What is this disaster
That has befallen us?"

Contemporary Song

Commentary

This song expresses cynicism about the state of modern India.
Vegetarian brahmins, who are forbidden to eat eggs, forget their
religious discipline as they go lusting after money. The rich indulge
themselves with their expensive toys while the poor are carried on
bamboo stretchers to the cremation grounds.

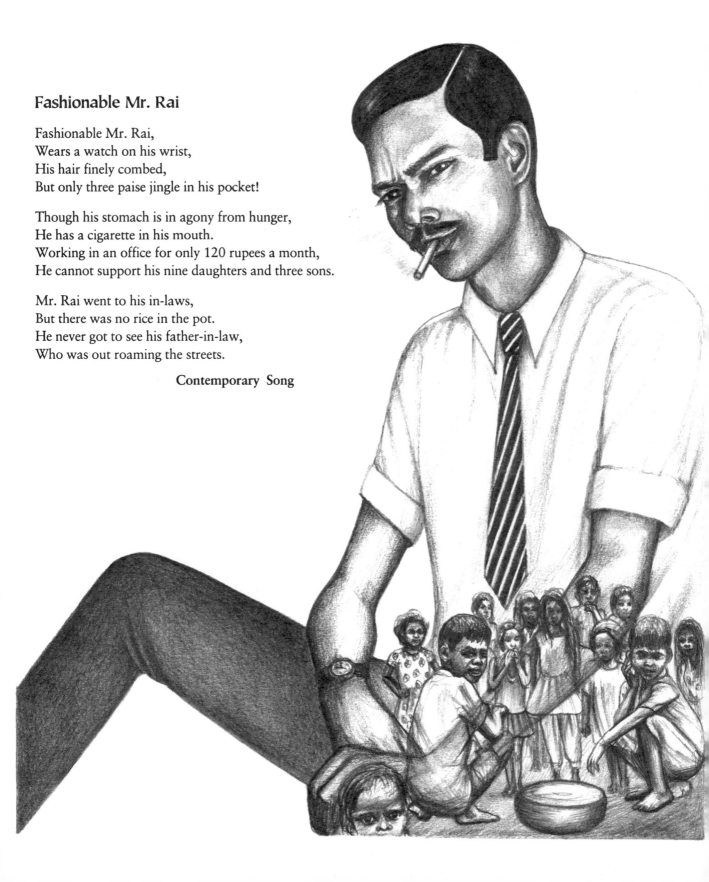

Fashionable Mr. Rai

Fashionable Mr. Rai,
Wears a watch on his wrist,
His hair finely combed,
But only three paise jingle in his pocket!

Though his stomach is in agony from hunger,
He has a cigarette in his mouth.
Working in an office for only 120 rupees a month,
He cannot support his nine daughters and three sons.

Mr. Rai went to his in-laws,
But there was no rice in the pot.
He never got to see his father-in-law,
Who was out roaming the streets.

Contemporary Song

The Ganja of Love

Come, come, O brothers!
All who want to smoke
The ganja of Love!
You will get intoxicated;
Your homes will be set aside.
Come, take shelter in Dharma.

With the sharp edge
Of discerning emotion,
Chop up the ganja
Which has been rubbed
With honeyed water
On a rosewood board.
Cut your passions with Love!

Fill up the chillum carefully,
Lest the ganja spill.
Don't make it without care;
Take heed of this advice.

Having wrung dry the safi-cloth,
Place it as a filter
Underneath the chillum.
Offer the first draw
As an invocation to the Guru;
Then smoke the ganja of Love!

Says Dina Panchanan:
"Can one who smokes the ganja of Love,
Really get high on anything else?"

Song of Dina Panchanan

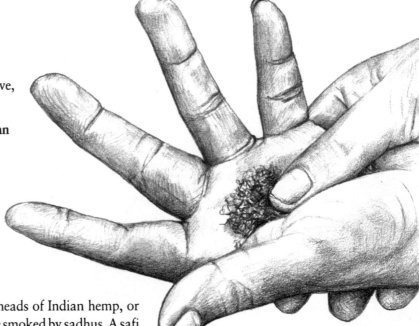

Commentary

Ganja is the leaves and dried flowering heads of Indian hemp, or
marijuana. A chillum is a conical clay pipe smoked by sadhus. A safi
is a cloth that is dampened, wrapped around the pipe stem, and used
as a cooling filter.

Why Blame Fate?

Why blame fate, O brother?
Having performed all your deeds,
You cry out for help!

That which is called fate or luck
Is wholly the creation of oneself.
With a vision of the Luminous Realms,
All such thoughts are cleansed.

By the power of knowledge and discernment,
Some people become kings;
Others stay as subjects.
Having fallen into the wrong path,
People say, "I have no luck."

Don't keep on blaming fate,
For all this is one's own creation.
With compassion, Lalan says:
"Duddu! You have no brains!"

Song of Duddu

13

Concealing Is Such a Terrible Thing

You will not get
This human body
Again and again.
Did you imagine that
No one came to know
Of your deeds
While on this earth?

Chitragupta has noted
All your actions.
Only He, the Supreme One
Can judge you.
In his presence.
There can be no cheating, no hiding.

You did not tell all;
Concealing is such a terrible thing.
Do not lie to the Man of the Heart,
For he has embraced you
With all His heart.

Go carefully,
Be aware!
The sun sets, darkness falls.
Man becomes God,
Then, a divine incarnation.
Says Bhava:
"Put your eyes together and see."

                                    Song of Bhava

Commentary

Chitragupta is the divine accountant who keeps the balance sheet of our karma. He is the keeper at Death's door and of Heaven's gates.

This Unknown Bird

Who is this unknown bird
That I have nurtured
Through my life,
Yet never came to know?

The bird speaks of Rama and Rahim;
She catches the Eternal Play.
Tell me, who knows her?
Oh, please tell me!

The bird's abode
Is in the corner of the eye.
Oh what a joy it is
To see her!
Who will dispel my infatuation?

If only she could recognize
The one with whom I return.
Says Lalan:
"How can I catch the Uncatchable
With such incompetence?"

Song of Lalan

Commentary

The bird, symbolizing the spirit of life, is mysterious and enchanting. It seduces but does not show its form, hiding in the depths of one's being. Rama is the seventh incarnation of Vishnu, as a hero; Rahim is an Arabic name of God.

When the Bird of Desire
Flies Away

The bird will fly away
When an ill wind hits the cage.

With the sides fallen down,
Where will the bird stand?
Now I sit and ponder;
A sudden shiver runs through me.

Whose is the cage?
Who is the bird?
How can one know the difference
Between one's own and another's?
For whom shall my tears pour?
The bird wants to make a fool of me!

Had I known before
That the wild cannot be tamed,
I would not have made love with Her!
Now I cannot see any way out.

"When the bird of desire flies away,
Only the empty cage will be left.
There will be no fellow traveler"
Says Lalan Fakir, crying.

Song of Lalan

I Cannot See Her Form

All my life I have taken care
Of an unknown bird.
She will not show me
Her unique form.
Tears stream from my eyes
In utter despair.

I can hear the sound of the bird,
But cannot see her form.
What should I do?
If I could only see her,
All my suffering would be dispelled.

I have been unable to know
This bird which I have nurtured for so long;
I shall never rid myself of the shame.
An awesome darkness looms ahead.
Who knows when the sensuous bird
Will fly away,
Flicking dust into my eyes?

The bird sits inside a cage.
It has nine doors.
Through which door does she fly
Both in and out,
Leaving me so confused?

Darbesh Siraj Sai says;
"Sit, Lalan, sit!
The trap is set before your eyes!"

Song of Lalan

Commentary

The cage is the body, and its nine doors are the nine apertures (two nostrils, two eyes, two ears, mouth, anus, and sex organ).

Those who are unaware of the presence of this inner spirit wander in labyrinths of sense experience, unable to catch the elusive bird, the spirit of life. Yogis believe that the divine spirit, though it is in the body, is beyond the realm of sense perception. To catch the bird, the trap is set at the "tenth gate"—the aperture at the back of the throat that connects the throat with the nasal passage.

The Mosquitoes of Passion

I have to leave this place
Because of the mosquitoes of passion.
They are humming and buzzing
Round and round my ears.

What is this sweet song
That makes my heart so restless?

With the Slap of Knowledge
I aim to kill the mosquitoes.
But the knowledge does not come;
The mosquitoes do not die.
I slap my face instead.

Finding this house with a broken door,
The mosquitoes are delighted.
Rules and etiquette
Hem in this abode of mine.

Having found the house abandoned,
The mosquitoes come in swarms.
Now that they suck my blood,
How can I save my life?

Commentary

The house refers to the body, and the broken door is a symbol of the imperfect organs of sense perception. When passion is directed only toward sense gratification, the vital energy is slowly removed from the body, since its flow is only outward.

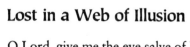

Lost in a Web of Illusion

O Lord, give me the eye salve of knowledge
And remove the darkness of ignorance.

O Guru, pierce my eye
With the needle of discernment
So that I may see the light.

I am a deluded being
Whose wanderings never cease.
I cannot find satisfaction
In this worldly life;
Remove my scar of pride.
O crazy heart,
I feel so ashamed,
Coming back to this world
Time and time again.

I have forgotten you, O Guru!
Lost in a web of illusion,
I wander through the myriad worlds.
Having fallen into this existence,
I die wandering.
Make me conscious, O Guru,
Through your precious grace.

Other than you, O Guru,
I have no one in this world.
I have heard from the scriptures
That you give refuge to the needy.
Give refuge to your servant Radha Shyam
And make him humble.

Song of Radha Shyam

The Guru Is Within the Body

While you are still conscious,
Recognize which house belongs to whom.
The Conscious Man resides within the body;
Sixteen doors to the eight rooms,
With a diamond door at the center.

The Guru is within the body.
Whose name do you recite?
Whose disciple have you become?
A disciple must always accept
The Guru's word as absolute.

Even when the world breaks up,
The Guru is here to stay.
Says Baul Darbesh:
"The essence is found
At the feet of the Guru.
Without his worship,
Life's journey is futile."

Commentary

The sixteen doors are the ten organs of perception and action
(ears, nose, eyes, tongue, skin, sex organ, anus, mouth, hands,
and feet) and the six delusions (anger, pride, envy, lust, greed,
and avarice). The eight rooms are the eyes, ears, mouth, nose,
throat, chest, anus, and hands.

O Wandering Heart

O wandering heart,
Take refuge at the feet of the Guru.
Why do you fear
The vast and boundless ocean?

Why do you want to drown
In a sea of sin?
What fear is there
When the ferryman is behind you?
By singing his praises
The heart becomes calmer.
O wandering heart!
You will go to Krishna's Paradise,
Laughing and dancing all the way.

Do not keep on saying:
"Mine, mine."
Closing your eyes,
You will see that all is dark.
As long as you have life,
Enjoy yourself.
Says Bhava:
"Why do you take the road to
   death?"

Song of Bhava

To Ride a Bicycle

If, O mind, you want to ride a bicycle,
First tie your loincloth well.
Then, with sincerity,
You will be sure to succeed.

Putting one foot on the pedal,
With a push and a hop, move forward.
All rituals and rites will vanish
Once you are standing on those pedals.
Keep your vision ahead;
Hold the handlebars steady.

Seated firmly on the bike, O mind,
Maintain your balance.
Breathing in, retain your breath.
Without looking to left or right,
Pedal on, reciting your mantra.

Be on the lookout for good roads;
Leave all pedantic arguments behind.
On becoming a Master,
Take the bicycle for a ride!
When inner and outer are united,
You will become an adept.
Then ring, O mind,
The bell of Discernment.

The sage Madhavananda floats effortlessly.
You, Bhavani, because of your karma,
Squeeze the brakes too hard
Riding at full speed;
Naturally you fall.
Such stupidity, O foolish one!

Song of Bhavani

The Ocean of
Myriad Forms

O mind, dive within and see
The ocean of myriad forms!
One who plunges into that ocean
Beholds the Form behind all forms.

All worldly forms are revealed,
To one who dives within.
Only the wise, in meditation,
See where forms arise
And how they float away.

O mind, you have not found out
Who you really are.
Look within, O mad one,
For the cause behind
These repeated births!
Says Rashid:
"Know that, O mind."

Song of Rashid

Give Him the Helm

River full of waves.
No one understands,
Steering their boats alone.

I wait for the Boatman
Who will ferry me across the river of Existence.
Oh, give him the helm,
Give him the helm.

Why do you hold the helm
When you don't know how to steer?
The Boatman of your mind
Has become intoxicated!
Tell him you have to cross the river
Before it is too late.

Mad Bhava was floating alone
In a broken boat,
Drowning, drowning.
Grasping the feet of the Boatman, he cried:
"Save me, save me!"

Song of Bhava

Take Me Across

If you have come
With the boat of your sacred name,
O Hari,
Then take me across!

I have neither riches,
Nor strength of devotion;
And have fallen down weak.

Speak to him,
You who are in the boat.
See if he will take me across.

"Oh, put me on the boat,"
I cry
From the other side in vain.
"Put me on the boat
As I sing his name!"

Ramanandadas says:
"I am unable to go across
Without catching that boat.
Put me on the boat
As I chant the Guru's name."

Song of Ramananda

The Tinker of Love

Here comes the Tinker of Love.
Come, come,
Exchange my broken pots for new!

From lack of Rasa
This pot has cracked
In nine places, not just one.
However much I mend it,
Not a single drop of Rasa remains!

Watching others fill up their pots
Makes me weep with sorrow.
How can I bear to see
A "living house" being burgled?

Commentary

Krishna is the Tinker of Love who mends the "pot," the sense-body, with his love potion. The mind, having become unsensual, loses whatever passion flows within from its search for sense-gratification. The nine cracks are the nine apertures of the body (two nostrils, two eyes, two ears, mouth, anus, and sex organ). The "living house" refers to the essential human spirit.

Don't Travel Third Class

Come let's go to Vrindaban
In the first class of discernment.
Get yourself a ticket, O Beloved.
Holding the feet of the Guru,
Travel on the route of Love.

Don't travel third class,
For you won't find a place to sit.
Those who have no faith in gurus
Are the unfortunate ones.
Pushing and fighting, O crazy brother,
They make such a racket.

Kunti's son is the Dharma ticket collector.
You feel his presence wherever you go.
The train goes straight through,
For all the lights are green.

At the rear there is the guard:
It is Shiva Himself.
Seeing the Three Attributes
He gives the signal to go.
The Blue-hued One spread his color
To make everything go blue.

First take the morning train
To the abode of Krishna.
Then go and touch the Guru's feet
If you want to catch the moon.

Commentary

Kunti is the mother of the five Pandava brothers in the Hindu epic the Mahabharata. Her eldest son, Yuddhistra, is the embodiment of Dharma, or law and righteousness. The Blue-hued One is Krishna.

The "Three Attributes" refers to *tamas, rajas,* and *sattva,* the three principles that shape the nature of the world. Tamas is the principle of inertia, rajas of activity, and sattva of intelligence and revelation.

Chaitanya's Train

Here comes Chaitanya's train
To Golden Nadia.
Radha's company has assembled
In the courtyard of Srivasa.

Sri Advaita is the ticket collector,
Nityananda the engineer.
Having become the driver,
Sri Gouranga drives the train through.

The poor and the suffering
Are so lucky;
No one is barred
Who has faith and virtue.
The tickets are easily obtained.

The rich wander about,
Unable to travel without tickets.
O foolish one,
Ramananda Rai has the tickets!

Says Sarad:
"Those who have Radha's blessing
Sit in first class
And go to the Eternal Abode."

Commentary

Chaitanya, or Gouranga, who is considered by many Bauls to be the original Baul, lived in the district of Nadia in West Bengal. His followers used to meet in the house of one of his most ardent disciples, Srivasa. Sri Advaita and Nityananda were two of Chaitanya's principal devotees. Ramananda Rai was an eminent scholar who became a follower of Chaitanya. The Eternal Abode is Krishna's paradise.

The Sensual Madman

A Sensual Madman has come
And caused chaos in Nadia.
Going with the mad one,
I too shall become mad.
I am a new follower
Of this luminous power.

Gour is mad, Nitai is mad,
And Advaita too is
A follower of this Madman.
Having become mad,
Sri Chaitanya has brought boatloads
Of the sacred name.

Brahma is mad, Vishnu is mad;
The other one cannot be caught.
Kailash's Shiva is mad.
He became mad
Tasting bhang and datura.

Commentary

The Sensual Madman is Chaitanya (also called Gour) of Nadia. Like Radha, he had an insatiable passion for the love of Krishna. Nitai and Advaita were two of his foremost disciples.

The "other one" is Shiva. According to Hindu myth, Shiva lives on Mount Kailash in the Himalayas. He is supposed to be intoxicated with bhang (a drink made from ground marijuana leaves) and datura (Jimson weed).

The Love-Garden of Krishna

My mind goes wandering
In the love-garden of Krishna.
There you will go
And surrender your heart
To a world of bliss.

The garden is guarded on all sides;
It stands in the sky.
That garden, O mad one,
Has no ground.
Brahma and Vishnu wait,
Hoping to explore it.

Five types of flowers
Eternally bloom in the garden.
Their fragrance is incomparable;
Their smell intoxicates the spirit.

In this garden of abundant fruits
There is one that is invisible.
Those who have tasted it
Become as if mad;
It fulfills their desires and ambitions.
Only those who have tasted it
Know its name.

Commentary

The love-garden of Krishna is the transcendental realm known as
Goloka. Even gods desire to explore this sensuous and magical
world. The five types of flowers represent the five devotional
sentiments (rasas). The invisible fruit is the Uncatchable Man, the
unseen form of Krishna.

Milkman of My Heart

O Milkman of my heart,
Give me milk twice a day.
This saying has worth;
Pure milk sinks to the bottom.

Don't keep the milk
In an open room,
For the jealous cat constantly roams.
Two ants, meeting each other, say:
"O mad one, how much can you drink
And how much will you spill?"

If you want to follow the saints,
Let the medicinal milk simmer effortlessly.
If you mix with sinners,
The milk turns sour.
How will you be able to drink it?

At home there is the Cow of Devotion.
Take care and serve Her well.
Take milk from her,
The one who grants
Whenever you ask.

Says Gosain:
"O Ananta,
The passionate calf
Breaks the rope.
Tether her well;
Stay close to her in one room."

Song of Ananta

Commentary

The Milkman and the cat both represent Krishna. The milk is a symbol of rasa, the passionate yearning of the devotee. The cow of devotion is Radha.

31
While There Is Still Passion

Prepare the rasa
While there is still passion
Within the body.
If you heat the rasa
With the fire of your passion,
It will surely thicken.

Let me tell you about rasa:
"Uncooked, it becomes sour.
Keeping the mind steady,
Stir the rasa,
So achieving the transformation."

Watch carefully.
Passion makes the rasa
Go round and round.
From passion comes
The seed of Love.

In the Love-dalliance,
Heat the rasa carefully.
Keep it covered
So it doesn't boil over,
For otherwise
All the work is wasted.

When choosing a good form
In which to set the rasa,
Remove all desires
For self-gratification.

The mind does all the preparation.
Business will be brisk,
Provided you are prepared.
Keep temptations under control,
For during this preparation
They become very powerful.

Learn the preparation of rasa,
By staying with a sensual sweet-seller.
Says Gosai Guru Chand to Radha Shyam:
"Learn this song of mine.
Having created the mood
Of Krishna's paradise,
Go, obtain the nectar!"

Song of Radha Shyam

Commentary

Here rasa refers to both sexual passion and devotional sentiments. By the heat of passion, the sexual energy is transformed from worldly passion into a divine erotic sentiment. With mindfulness, rasa is controlled and transformed.

The song uses the analogy of boiling milk to explain the process of transforming sexual energy. In the fire of passion, mundane sense-experience "evaporates," leaving behind the essence—the seed of love. The uncooked milk symbolizes raw passion. If passion is too strong and there is a lack of mental awareness and control, the sexual fluids "boil over," like the milk. On the other hand, even divine sentiments become sour, like uncooked milk, and are wasted if passion is absent. By gradually transforming the raw sexual energy into a sublime experience of divine emotion, one achieves all the richness and wealth of Krishna's paradise.

A sweet-seller, through years of experience, knows the preparation of milk sweets. Here the sensual sweet-seller is the Guru, who assumes the nature of a woman to teach the secrets of sexual yoga.

To Catch the Uncatchable

Does everyone know of that
    emotion,
Which binds Krishna to the Gopis?
Only bees, with pure rasa,
Know of the Love of the Gopis.
On seeing Lord Krishna,
Gopis lose all thoughts
Of sin or redemption.

Those who become like gopis
Know the atmosphere
Of Krishna's playground.
Only *they* really know
How to catch the Uncatchable.

The Transient Being changes;
The Immortal is changeless.
Does the mere knowledge of that
Make one dwell in the rasa?
Says Lalan:
"I am overwhelmed,
Cooking this rasa."

Song of Lalan

To Be a Fired Pot

You are unable to keep the love-water
In your unfired pot.
If you put an unfired pot into water,
It soon dissolves;
The couple starts to quarrel!

If you want to be a fired pot,
Then go to the Guru's house.
There, in the fire of love,
You will become strong,
Your spirit will begin to sparkle.

Sadananda, having thought thus,
Become an Aul.
"O Manohar,
When will you become a Baul?"
By husking grain, one gets rice;
O crazy one,
What do you get
From husking the husk?

Song of Sadananda

Commentary

The pot symbolizes the body, which enshrines the spirit. The unfired pot
is the body that has yet to go through the rigors of yogic discipline and is
unable to retain sexual passion owing to a lack of self-control. At another
level, this song refers to the sexual-yogic practices of the Bauls. The
"Guru's house" refers to the yoni of woman. The Auls are one of the
subsects of Hindu Bauls.

34

The Blossoming Does Not End

The lotus of the heart
Has continued to bloom
Through eons and eons.
It keeps us bound together;
What can I do?

It keeps on blossoming,
Blossoming, blossoming . . .
The blossoming does not end.

There is honey in this flower,
Whose rasa is unique;
The greedy bee cannot leave it
Because it is so sweet.

This is why
You and I
Are bound together.
Oh, where can I find Liberation?

Commentary

Bauls do not seek liberation from worldly life. They revel in the
ecstasies of sublime joys. Honey is the symbol of feminine passion, and
the bee is the enjoyer of that passion.

Dive Within and See!

Don't speak of emotions
To the insensitive.
Don't tell anyone,
For no one will understand.
By soaking coal in milk,
You cannot make it white!

A certain king desired
That bitter should become sweet.
He fed a neem tree
With sackfuls of sugar.
The tree became three times as
    bitter;
Never did it acquire any sweetness.

If you keep a parrot and a crow
Together in the same cage,
Taking great care,
Feeding them butter and cheese,
In the hope that both will speak,
The parrot quickly learns to talk;
The crow never will.

A poor man from the jungle
Stood in front of the king's house.
Feeling compassionate,
The king gave him a coconut to
    drink.
But the man bit into that coconut
And broke his teeth.
He did not think
Of cracking it open.

Through the City of Emotion
A large river flows.
O mind,
You have not dived into it
Since birth!

Having forgotten Hiruchand's
    words,
You have become bitter.
Humble Panja says:
"Dive within and see.
You will surely find the pearl!"

Song of Panja Saha

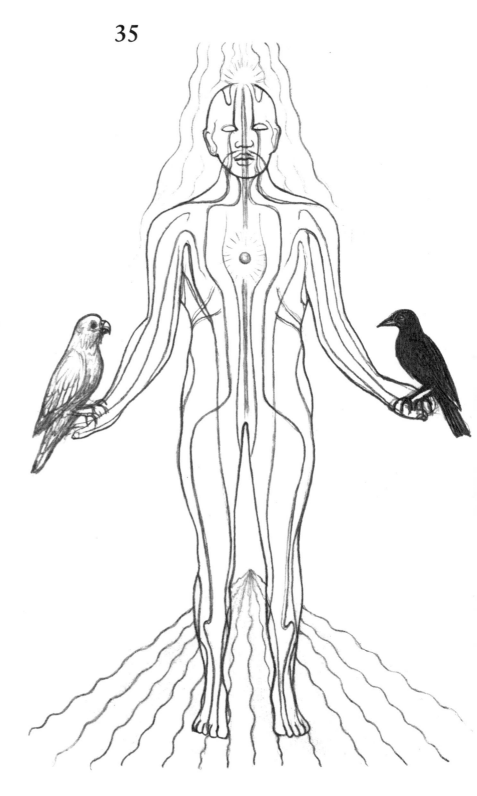

Commentary

The neem is a medicinal tree with a very bitter taste. The
City of Emotion is the human body, and the "large river"
is the life-current that flows within.

Tell Me

When there was no sky, wind, or clouds,
There was no sun or Moon,
No Brahma, Vishnu, or Shiva.

Tell me how
From the formless void
Form came.
Tell me, O Compassionate One,
How at that time
Purusha and Prakriti took shape.

What is the meaning
Of the Original Word?
What are its attributes?
What elements does it contain?
Are the entwined attributes
Conscious or unconscious?

Says Sarad:
"I sit here wondering
From where this world came.
Tell me, O Guru,
Who is the Lord of Creation?"

Song of Sarad

Commentary

In this song Sarad Baul ponders the mystery of creation. Purusha is the supreme consciousness, the unchanging, eternal presence behind all existence; Prakriti is the active force of nature that forms and moves the world. On another level, Purusha refers to man and Prakriti to woman.

All Have the Nature
of Woman

O mind, are you man or woman?
I cannot understand
This marvelous secret.

From the lips of sadhus
I hear that Mother Nature,
Seeing the Indivisible Spirit,
Created the universe
From within herself.
That is why it is said:
"Within the universe
All have the nature of woman,
Not man."

There is only one Indivisible Spirit;
The Eternal Krishna.
May Kangal, aspiring with yoga,
Realize in joyous ecstasy,
The mind as woman!

Song of Kangal

Commentary

In Baul metaphysics, the masculine represents the static aspect of the universe and the feminine represents the dynamic and creative force. As everything within the universe is subject to change, all its elements have the feminine aspect. The Bauls see the mind as feminine because it exists in a dynamic universe, changing and moving, creating and destroying itself. Only Krishna, the Supreme Being, the changeless one, is beyond the cycle of birth and death.

Mere Talking Is Not Enough

To be a devotee,
Mere talking is not enough.
One who so desires
Should be a follower of Shakti.

When Shakti manifests,
Worldly ways are destroyed.
Conquer the passions
By sacrificing all delusions.

When passion is controlled,
Wisdom begins to blossom.
In this effortless way,
Occult powers are obtained.

Having obtained powers,
The mind assumes a tranquil
     nature;
All jealousy is removed.
When the mind becomes discerning,
True devotion begins to dawn.

Says Kangal:
"When devotion appears,
There is no sense of separateness
     anymore;
Creation and dissolution cease to be.
The pure awakened consciousness,
Realizes the nature of the Absolute."

Song of Kangal Fakir

Commentary

Bauls do not believe in blind faith. They are devoted only to that which they can experience directly. To know the truth, the mind must be discerning. For it to be discerning, it must possess acute mental faculties by which it can both perceive and judge. These mental faculties must be able to penetrate beyond immediate reality by means of occult powers. Only then does the mind see behind the facade of appearances, into the causal worlds. These powers are gained through meditation and rigorous yogic practice. The yogi experiences spiritual consciousness by awakening Kundalini, the primal manifestation of Shakti, the creative and dynamic force of the cosmos.

Don't Beat Woman, O Brother

O mind, in which mood
Will you do your sadhana?
First, become a devotee of woman;
For the world is encircled by her.
Only the Guru is awake!

A woman's wealth is not mundane;
It illuminates the whole world.
At her feet I have seen
The light of a million moons.
Without woman there can be
No spiritual enjoyment.

If a person gets a silver coin,
He touches it to his forehead.
How much lustrous gold and silver
Does he place at her feet?
If you don't recognize
The real wealth of woman,
You will surely suffer in sin.

Don't beat woman, O brother.
When you beat her, you beat the Guru!
The sage Chaitanya has spoken
Of her bashful nature.
Go, place your head at her feet.
By the power of this vision,
All sufferings will be dispelled.

Song of Panja Saha

Commentary

"How can one renounce woman?" Bauls ask. She is the living force that sustains life. In the second stage of the Bauls' spiritual discipline, the guru-principle is feminine, for it is "woman" who reveals the mysteries of the universe.

In Hindu tradition, when a mendicant receives a coin from a householder, it will be touched to the forehead as a sign of respect to the giver. The song suggest that women should be so honored.

The Mother of All Beings

Put the feet of woman
Upon your head;
For without her,
Nothing moves!

Renouncing woman to become a hermit
Makes one a monkey of a renunciate.
Haven't you noticed
That all the holy shrines
Are at the feet of woman?

She is the Wish-granting Tree
Of which I hear in the sadhu traditions.
Having stumbled on orthodox teachings,
I fail to have a glimpse of her.

In the form of the woman of the house,
She is the Mother of all beings.
In her sensuous aspect
She fulfills all wishes.
Duddu sings her song,
Which he has just composed.

Song of Duddu

Commentary

In Bengal the Divine is more often viewed in Its feminine aspect, as the dynamic power of change and evolution. Without the grace of woman, no spiritual progress is possible. One must become aware of her all-pervasive nature: first by perceiving the physical body of woman as a divine incarnation, and then by realizing the feminine principle within oneself. Since the main spiritual practices of the Bauls are sexual, male Bauls do not renounce woman even in the final stage of discipline, that of the renunciate. The "Wish-granting Tree" (symbol of the transformed life-energies within the subtle body) is, in Hindu mythology, one of the ornaments and attributes of Mount Kailash, the Eternal Abode of the true yogic couple. Mount Kailash is also a symbol of the Axis Mundi.

Be Like a Woman

O mind, be like a woman!
Assuming the nature of woman,
Practice your sadhana.
The body's passion will rise.

Take the dweller of the six-petaled lotus
Up the "inverse path."
Light will burst forth
When it reaches the eye between the eyes.
Afflictions will be dispelled;
The flow of passion will be steadied.
Krishna will assume his Form.
The Guru's image will dawn.

Take the dweller of the root lotus
To the thousand-petaled one.
United with her, you will cross
To the shores of freedom.
That youthful, sensual, ecstatic maiden
Gives such sweet honey;
Krishna Himself appears!

First catch the "image"
Within the Universal Form.
There you will see
The light of a million suns.
The Guru will not go away,
O ignorant one!
Krishna's grace is bestowed
By the Guru's compassion.

Song of Rupachand

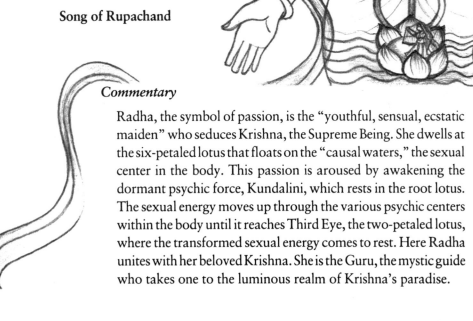

Commentary

Radha, the symbol of passion, is the "youthful, sensual, ecstatic maiden" who seduces Krishna, the Supreme Being. She dwells at the six-petaled lotus that floats on the "causal waters," the sexual center in the body. This passion is aroused by awakening the dormant psychic force, Kundalini, which rests in the root lotus. The sexual energy moves up through the various psychic centers within the body until it reaches Third Eye, the two-petaled lotus, where the transformed sexual energy comes to rest. Here Radha unites with her beloved Krishna. She is the Guru, the mystic guide who takes one to the luminous realm of Krishna's paradise.

The Living Kali

You have not seen the living Kali
In the midst of your home;
Worshiping dolls and idols
Has made you blind!

Without knowing Her living form,
Tell me, O dear one,
What have you found,
Prostrating yourself on a straw mat?

Hindus are such fools;
Unable to see Her in woman,
They worship dolls
Night and day.
If you want to see Her,
Try dying!

No one has learned to recognize
That Shakti,
The Primordial Power
Which creates all phenomena.
From the center of the universe,
Duddu asks:
"What form is the Mother of all beings?"

Commentary

The living Kali within the home represents the feminine energy that exists within all human beings. The goddess Kali is called Shakti because it is by her power that the universe is created. She is the awesome dark goddess who "consumes" human consciousness, leaving nothing but the corpse of the ego resting on the "fire" of time. "Dying" here refers to the conscious act of severance from one's psychological conditioning and ego-clinging; in a sexual context, it refers to ejaculation and physical orgasm.

To Control Your Mind

If you want to control your mind,
Form a group of bandits.
As long as there is illusion,
You cannot steal,
And get caught wherever you go.
Tearing the web of illusion,
Practice your spiritual disciplines.

A mad one says:
"The day has passed by;
Now I dress as a thief.
Stealing is a great art
If you do not get caught."

The entire wealth of Shiva,
Lies at the crimson feet of Kali.
Steal it in broad daylight!

Commentary

The "bandits" are the six delusions (anger, pride, envy, lust, avarice, and greed). Shiva, the symbol of transcendental existence, lies at the feet of the goddess Kali, the creator of all changing phenomena and illusion.

Compassion

The light has shone in the sky;
At last, compassion begins to
   flow.
Waking up in the morning,
I see before my very eyes
Compassion flooding down.

Flowers shower down;
Birds fly away;
Leaves are wet with dew.
The moonlit night melts
In the heat of the morning sun.

Ishan cries,
"O Compassionate Moon!"
For his pain is deep.

Song of Ishan Fakir

Only the Heart Knows

Only the heart knows its crazy ways.
Only my Guru knows of it.
Chilies grow on bamboo trees;
Gourds on eggplant stalks.
Only the heart knows its crazy ways.

In the morning was the betrothal;
At noon the wedding took place.
The wife came home in the evening
With a child in her arms.
Only the heart knows its crazy ways.

The plow tills the river banks;
The bull is in the calf's womb.
When the peasant was born,
His food was left in the fields.
Only the heart knows its crazy ways.

There is no water in the sea,
But waves break in the marketplace.
When the father was not yet born,
The son had a bride on his lap.
Only the heart knows its crazy ways.

A fakir came from distant lands;
A torn blanket covered the sky.
Where will I bury him
When he dies?
Only the heart knows its crazy ways.

The Love-Market

To whom shall I speak of love, O friend?
Talking of love to people
Makes me mad with joy.

I went to make love
In the love-market.
Six thieves pounced on me
And pushed me deep into trouble.
On trying to run away,
I found myself quite helpless.

The lover of love
Makes love effortlessly.
Love-sick Bilvamangal
Went to Chinta's house
And climbed up the snake-rope
To get over the wall.
What fear had he of death?

Chandidas and Rajakini
Are the crowning Jewels of Love;
In one death,
They both died.
What death have I had?

Vaidyanath, having thought thus, says:
"My days pass in turmoil.
One should sing the Guru's praise
And honor him;
Otherwise, how will your death be blessed?"

Song of Vaidyanath

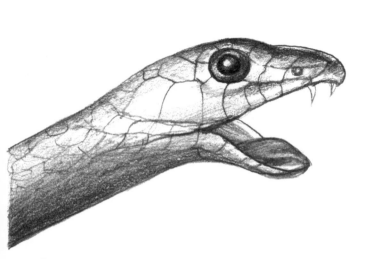

Commentary

The six thieves of the love-market are the six delusions that limit the experience of love (lust, pride, anger, envy, greed, and avarice). Bilvamangal, the hero of an eighteenth-century Bengali play, was so consumed with love for his beloved, Chinta, that one night he crossed a raging river on what he thought was a floating log; it was actually a corpse. Later, he climbed up her garden wall by holding on to a snake, thinking it to be a rope.

Chandidas and Rajakini are another example of passionate love in Bengali literature. According to one legend, Chandidas was separated from Rajakini and killed. When she heard about it, she ran to the cremation grounds where his body had been taken. Chandidas rose from death on the funeral pyre and beckoned to Rajakini. Together they danced on the fire as their united spirits ascended to the heavens. The image of dying together is also a symbol of simultaneous orgasm.

My House

Someone else has the key to my house.
How will I get to see its wealth?

In my house there are bags of gold,
Yet others do the buying and selling;
I was born blind and cannot see.

If the lady at the door is willing,
She will leave it open.
Unable to recognize her,
I wander about in dark alleys.

Inside this man, O mind,
There is the Jewel Man.
In spite of having the jewel,
I cannot see it.

Song of Lalan

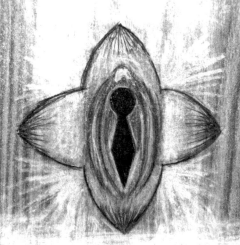

Commentary

Bauls believe that Truth resides within the self and that those who search for spiritual wealth in the external world wander blindly. To find the Jewel Man, the Supreme Being, one must enter the "house of treasures"—the body. The door of this "house" is the yoni of the "woman within," the entrance to the central channel of subtle energy at the root lotus through which Kundalini, the cosmic power, makes her entrance.

The Ocean of Myriad Forms

Some float and others drown
When they dive into the ocean
Of myriad forms.

Only those who know
How to catch snakes
Can get the jewel.
Finding the jewel,
They become rich.
The insensitive,
Unable to take it,
Fall down poisoned.

The jewel is in the depths
Of the fathomless waters.
The diver, descending,
Picks it up.
Can others, by holding their breath,
Dive within and retrieve the jewel?

As passion is mixed with love,
So water is with milk.
A sensual swan,
With graceful skill,
Can discard the water
And drink only the milk.

Song of Nitya Khepa

Commentary

The "ocean of myriad forms" represents the causal waters out of which all forms arise. In the human body this refers to the sexual center below the navel. According to Indian mythology, there is a snake in the causal waters that has a jewel on its head. The snake is a symbol of passion, and the jewel is its transformed and crystallized form, the experience of love.

In Hinduism, swans are said to have the unique ability to separate milk from water. Thus, the swan is the symbol of a discerning yogi who is able to separate lust from love. Water symbolizes the solar breath which flows through the right nostril, and milk is the lunar breath which flows through the left nostril. The warmth of the sun enhances passion, and from the coolness of the moon, the nectar of love showers down.

The Jewel and the Snake

There is a jewel on the snake's head,
Yet how many have found it?
The jewel is obtained
By taming the snake;
Snake poison can kill a man.

The snake looks harmless.
It is cold to touch,
Its nature is cunning and deceitful;
Its venom is lethal.
By the snake's breath
All beings are destroyed;
Even a strong mind is weakened.

How can I find the jewel?
I don't know the sacred teachings.
In the darkness of ignorance
I go to catch the snake.

The jewel can only be found
By the Guru's grace.
The Living Jewel will be given
With loving care,
By the nymphs of Braja.
At the ninth stage of life
The jewel begins to appear.
By the tenth,
Its manifestation is complete.

Song of Nitya Khepa

Commentary

According to Indian mythology, there is a jewel on the head of the snake that lies below the "causal waters." The snake is both a symbol of raw passion and of Kundalini, the latent cosmic force in all beings; the jewel is the transformed aspect of passion, the pure and clear experience of love. It represents the crystallization of spiritual endeavors. This passion, however, is highly dangerous, and only those who are spiritually and emotionally mature are able to enjoy its myriad delights. Whoever wishes to have a vision of Krishna, the Living Jewel, must go through ten ascending stages or "steps" of spiritual evolution. Finally, when one has become like the Gopis, passionate and self-sacrificing, the luminous vision of Krishna appears.

Braja is the region around Vrindaban, Krishna's legendary "playground."

Falling in Love

Is it easy to make love?
First put aside individuality;
Then you and I will fall in love
This very lifetime.

Intoxicated with love,
The Man of Divine Emotion
Always floats on the ocean of love.
In the true love of Krishna,
All lust is removed.

Without knowing the nature of emotions,
Falling in love is like a snake
Catching a muskrat;
From greed, he sins.
From sin, he dies.
He goes to the kill, but dies instead!

Nectar in the moon,
Honey in the lotus;
Tell me how they can be united.
The moon in the sky;
The lotus in the lake.
Having made the hive,
The bee stores honey in it.

The union of moon and lotus
Is by the act of Divine Love alone.
Where there is real passion,
There is Divine Love.
See it by observing well!
Milk becomes butter by churning.

"In the movable house,
Is the Immovable Man.
In the moving, the stationary;
In the stationary, the moving."
So says Ramanandadas to Bhava.

Song of Bhava

Commentary

Bauls believe that passion manifests itself either as lust or as love. Lust leads to deprivation of the senses, while love leads to a heightening of sensual pleasure. The snake (symbol of male sexual passion) is tempted at the sight of the muskrat (symbol of female sexuality) and out of sheer greed goes to eat it. The muskrat, however, is poisonous and must therefore be treated with great care.

The nectar in the moon is the pure love of Krishna, and the honey in the lotus is the erotic passion of Radha. Within passion is the seed of love. The image of milk becoming butter through the process of churning represents the yogic process by which sexual passion is transformed into love.

The "movable house" is the human body, which enshrines the divine spirit, the Immovable Man.

To Know "Another"

If you don't know your "own" mind,
How can you know "another's"?
Knowing "another's" makes her your "own."
In good faith, she will become as yours.

Have the desire to know "another";
Clinging fast to self-knowledge,
Turn the without within.
Then you will befriend the Uncatchable.

When you see the Spiritual Man,
You will feel content in his presence.
The mind will not drown
In the well of thought,
When it rests at the Silver Feet.

Says Mad Kalachand:
"I have heard that he can be found
Near the honey bowl.
How can I find it
Without faith or the Guru's grace?"

Song of Kalachand

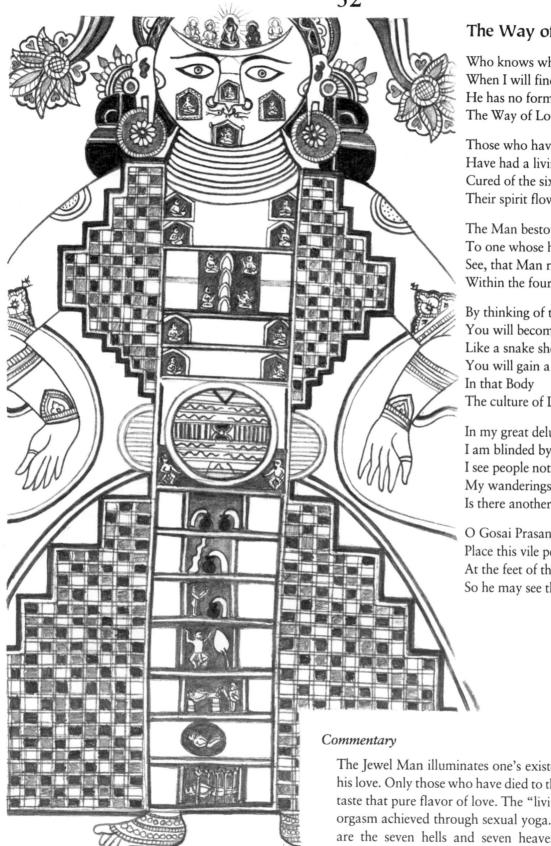

The Way of Love

Who knows when that day will come
When I will find the Jewel Man?
He has no form;
The Way of Love is His manifestation.

Those who have tasted the flavor of love
Have had a living death;
Cured of the six ailments,
Their spirit flows on.

The Man bestows grace
To one whose heart cries out for him.
See, that Man resides
Within the fourteen worlds.

By thinking of the Man
You will become him;
Like a snake shedding its skin,
You will gain a Body of Bliss.
In that Body
The culture of Love flourishes.

In my great delusion
I am blinded by the light of day.
I see people not as one, but many.
My wanderings have not finished;
Is there another as naughty as I?

O Gosai Prasaneri Das,
Place this vile person's desires
At the feet of the Guru,
So he may see the Inner Man.

Song of Hari

Commentary

The Jewel Man illuminates one's existence with the light of his love. Only those who have died to the bondage of the ego taste that pure flavor of love. The "living death" is the great orgasm achieved through sexual yoga. The fourteen worlds are the seven hells and seven heavens, all of which are conceived of as within the body.

To Play a Game of Cards

You came into this world
To play a game of cards.
Now know that the one Brahma
Is the meaning of the Ace.

The body's five elements
Are symbolized by the fifth card;
The six delusions by the sixth.
If you look within,
You will also find the seven stories.

You will understand
The meaning of the eighth card
When you get to know
The eight rooms within this body;
The body's nine doors
You will find in the ninth.

One who becomes a knave of the body,
Vanquishes all.
Fearing no one,
He goes by himself.

O Gyanananda,
What have you done?
You came to play a game of cards
And lost!
The fifth and the sixth
Have you bound for life!

Song of Gyananda

Commentary

In this modern song, life is seen as a gamble; only the truly aware are able to "win." Brahma is the creator. The body's five elements are earth, water, air, fire, and "ether" or space. The six delusions are anger, pride, envy, lust, greed, and avarice. The seven stories are the seven heavens, or the seven levels of consciousness. The eight rooms are the eyes, ears, mouth, nose, throat, chest, anus, and hands. The nine doors are the nine apertures of the body (two eyes, two ears, two nostrils, mouth, anus, and sex organ).

The Three-Storied House

Eight rooms, nine doors;
Without any locks,
This house is three-storied.

Upstairs there is the court
And in between, the marketplace.
Downstairs the workers meditate
On the garland of Love.

Nine guards constantly move
Around the nine doors;
When they are awake,
The six bandits steal.

You will go in peace
By turning the key to the House of Jewels;
Peacefully you will go to sleep.

Commentary

The three-storied house is the body, the microcosm in which all
the activities of the macrocosm are found. In the higher centers
of consciousness, the mind makes the judgments, and in the
lower centers, passion and love both work and play. Between
the higher and lower centers, there is a constant flow of spiritual
wealth. For the symbolism of the numbers eight, nine, and six,
see commentary on song 53.

Secrets of the Body

Know the secrets of the body.
How can you find the essence outside,
When it is within all the time?

The egg and the seed
Are the parents two.
Why not worship the seed,
The forefather of us all?

Keeping Kundalini as a companion,
Hoist up the sail of the mind.
By making disciples
Of the ten organs of perception and action,
Lift them with the fishing line of knowledge.

Know the secret of the 24½ moons
From the precious Guru.
Says Gosai Chand:
"The Guru's treasures
Are in the Spiritual Body."

Song of Gosai Chand

Commentary

The central concept of Baul philosophy, that of "truth within the body," assumes that the spiritual search begins and ends within oneself and that to seek for spiritual knowledge in the external world is folly. One inherits the qualities of the physical and psychological body from one's parents, but the spiritual body, which is eternal, is the root cause of existence.

Kundalini is the latent spiritual power within. The ten organs of perception and action consist of the five organs of sense perception (ears, eyes, tongue, nose, and skin) and the five organs of action (sex organs, anus, hands, feet, and mouth).

The 24½ moons are the points in the body that become sensitive ("lit up") during the sexual act. They include the ten fingernails, ten toenails, two cheeks, lower lip, and tongue. The half moon is on the forehead, the location of the "Third Eye" of all-seeing consciousness.

The Trap

O crazy heart,
There is a mouse trap—a human trap—
At the center of the universe.
No one is pushed into this trap;
Everyone falls through their own desires.

Such is the magic of this trap;
It grasps with so much strength
That even the three worlds collapse.
The lustful and the greedy fall into it.
Unable to get out, they lose their lives.

The trap faces downward.
Oh, how can I speak of it?!
Having fallen into it,
I suffer all my life.
I have lost my spiritual path
Having fallen into this trap.

Even Brahma does not know
The workings of this trap.
Whether Shiva knows or not,
That I cannot say.
How can mortals have the knowledge
Which even Shiva does not possess?

Commentary

The mouse trap, the human trap, is man's own heart. The six
delusions entrap humans, leaving them crying for liberation. Besides
the general symbolism of this song, there is a more particular one.
The trap that faces downward is the yoni, the source of passion.
Even Brahma, the creator of the universe, could not control his
passion upon seeing the beauty of his own daughter, who was
incarnated as a sacred cow. Shiva is a paradox. He is both the
Supreme Ascetic and the Enjoyer of all forms of sensual pleasure.

The Magical Machine

Having put in the coal
I close my furnace gate;
The fire burns
By the power of the breath.
This train is driven by a magical machine.

The engineer, in this room,
Is dying in Waves of Bliss;
Through this telephone, the news travels
Wherever the mind wishes.
Kulakundalini, the Empress,
Rests in the four-petaled lotus.

In Manipur station,
The skilled drive their trains in solitude
Wherever their minds choose to go.
Sixteen beings guard this express train.

When the wind room is closed,
The engineer will escape.
With the worldly train left standing,
The passengers will walk away.
Says Gosain Pramananda:
"Being repelled,
They will go away."

Song of Gosain Pramananda

Commentary

Bauls often use images from contemporary life to depict ancient concepts. In this song, the dynamics of a train engine are used as an allegory for the body. The yogic practice of breathing to achieve spiritual transformation is compared to the hot engine room of a coal-powered train. The engineer is the Guru or the Man of the Heart, who sports in the fire of passion. Kulakundalini is the primordial power that rests at the lowest center of consciousness, the four-petaled lotus at the base of the spine. Manipur is a town in Assam (the original bastion of Tantra) in the far-eastern corner of India and also refers to the ten-petaled lotus above the sexual center. The sixteen beings who guard the train are the six delusions (anger, pride, envy, lust, greed, and avarice) and the ten organs of perception and action (see commentary on song 55).

The Light of Many Colors

What wick is in this lamp
That burns in the City
Both night and day?
It burns in the center of the lamp.
See it, O beloved ones!
No winds or rain will make it flicker.

If you pinch the wick,
The lamp burns without oil.
Those who know this truth
Light it this way.
Can others light it so?

Such is the nature of the light
That even the blind,
In darkness, see.
This light of many colors
Burns radiantly
Throughout the entire universe.

Dina Punya, in despair, says:
"The light saves the City;
Know that when this light goes out,
The City will not survive!"

Song of Dina Punya

Commentary

The braided lamp wick is composed of the three channels of subtle energy that run through the spinal column. The light that burns at the Third Eye, the lamp, illuminates the entire microcosm, symbolized by the City. This is the light of the Supreme Being.

The three subtle channels merge at the Third Eye. Beyond is the eternal realm where there is no change. Only an adept yogi is able to fuse together the energies within these channels.

Light from a Jewel

From where does the radiant light come
That shines above the two petals?
Light from a jewel
Bursts forth abundantly!

Full of light is this Eternal Realm,
In which the whole of Creation resides.
Having reached the two-petaled lotus,
Everything becomes known;
No obstacles remain.

Between the hundred-petaled lotus
And the thousand-petaled one,
Rasa and Rati move to and fro.
At the twin petals they rest
In the form of lightning.
At the six-petaled lotus,
Their play evokes a new life.

The Six Truths manifest
At the six-petaled lotus.
From the ten-petaled lotus,
The river Ganges gently flows.
One who is at Her banks,
Knows her Divine Qualities.
So says Lalan,
As taught by his Guru.

Song of Lalan

Commentary

The light that radiates from above the two-petaled lotus is
Goloka, the Eternal Realm of Radha-Krishna. In the human
microcosm this is in the thousand-petaled lotus in the crown of
the head. Radha, the symbol of the essence of rasa, the passionate
erotic energy, rests on the primeval waters. Below is a hundred-
petaled lotus. Krishna, the symbol of rati, is the crystallized
essence of love. His abode is the thousand-petaled lotus. Through
their union, they invoke the power of love, which is likened to
lightning. The "Six Truths" are the six delusions (lust, pride,
anger, envy, greed, and avarice). Those who can overcome these
delusions while in a passionate state are able to go through the
fire of the ten-petaled lotus, which is above the six-petaled lotus.
Having gone through it, the yogi bathes in the cool waters of the
Ganges.

When the Eye Is Consecrated

If you want to see the Golden Man,
Come closer!
Know the four principles
Of *Nachut, Lahut, Malkut,* and *Jabarut.*

At the three banks of Triveni,
The Uncatchable Man comes and goes.
He shimmers as he rises,
Like the waxing and waning of the
    moon.

The man moves through the house
Of eighteen rooms.
He always rides upon the breath,
Coming in and out.

Bakher Saha Fakir says:
"Listen, O brother,
When the eye is consecrated,
The Man can be seen dancing and
    playing.
Residing in the lotus of the heart,
He shimmers like the radiant moon."

Song of Bakher Saha

Commentary

In this song, Sufi and Sahajiya concepts are integrated. *Nachut, Lahut, Malkut,* and *Jabarut* are Sufi terms for the physical, psychological, psychic, and spiritual worlds, corresponding to the body, the conscious mind, the unconscious, and the divine realms. The Uncatchable Man is the highest consciousness of Love, which comes down to the physical plane, the yoni—the "three banks of Triveni"—during the menstrual period. The eighteen rooms in the body are the seven heavens and seven hells of Hindu mythology and the four worlds of the Sufis mentioned above.

The Path of Emotion

The Golden Man is floating
On rasa.
One who knows the Path of Emotion
See him easily.

The river of 360 flavors
Flows through the cosmos.
In it, the form of the Man
Shines eternally.

He has no trace of parentage;
He socializes with unfamiliar company.
Owing to his yoga practice
In the causal waters,
His comings and goings are mysterious.

To the one who wishes
To see the full moon
At the time of the new moon,
Lalan says:
"Always remain seated at the banks
Where the three rivers meet."

Song of Lalan

Commentary

The Golden Man floats on a sea of sensual delights. In this song, rasa refers to the erotic sentiment as a divine experience. It is believed that during menstruation (the new moon), the Golden Man comes down from his natural abode in the two-petaled lotus to the sexual region below the navel, which the Bauls call the "causal waters." He travels in the Shushumna, the central channel of subtle energy, the river of 360 "flavors" (see commentary on song 62). The banks where the three rivers meet are at the yoni, where three types of menstrual fluid flow. The Man is like the luminous full moon that lights up the dark mysterious night. He has no trace of parentage, for he was not born in the causal world; his ways are effortless, spontaneous, unpredictable, and full of surprises.

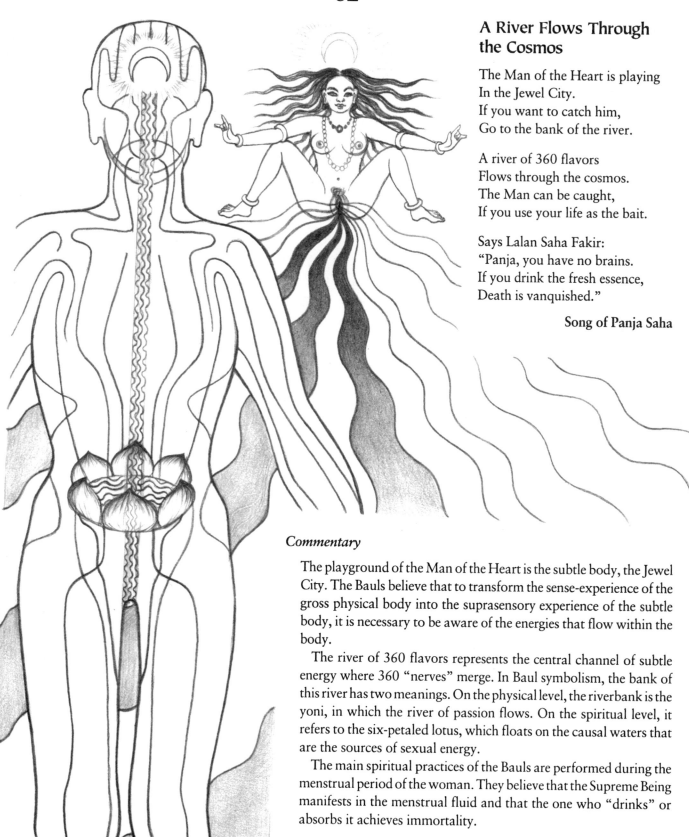

A River Flows Through the Cosmos

The Man of the Heart is playing
In the Jewel City.
If you want to catch him,
Go to the bank of the river.

A river of 360 flavors
Flows through the cosmos.
The Man can be caught,
If you use your life as the bait.

Says Lalan Saha Fakir:
"Panja, you have no brains.
If you drink the fresh essence,
Death is vanquished."

Song of Panja Saha

Commentary

The playground of the Man of the Heart is the subtle body, the Jewel City. The Bauls believe that to transform the sense-experience of the gross physical body into the suprasensory experience of the subtle body, it is necessary to be aware of the energies that flow within the body.

The river of 360 flavors represents the central channel of subtle energy where 360 "nerves" merge. In Baul symbolism, the bank of this river has two meanings. On the physical level, the riverbank is the yoni, in which the river of passion flows. On the spiritual level, it refers to the six-petaled lotus, which floats on the causal waters that are the sources of sexual energy.

The main spiritual practices of the Bauls are performed during the menstrual period of the woman. They believe that the Supreme Being manifests in the menstrual fluid and that the one who "drinks" or absorbs it achieves immortality.

The Spiraling Tube

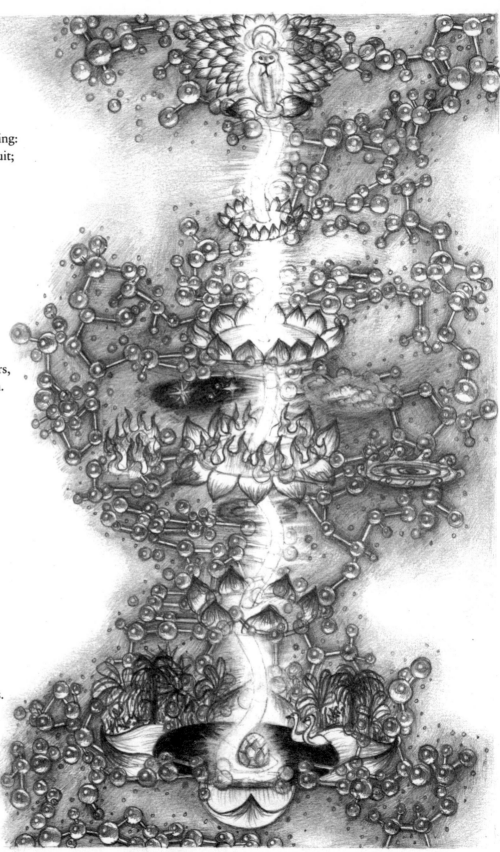

The Man is playing
In the spiraling tube.
The five elements
Surrounding the ten-petaled lotus
Are tough indeed!

This country has a paradoxical saying:
"The flower eats the head of the fruit;
From the phantasmagorical tree,
The creeper hangs ablaze."
Where the moon lights the day
And the sun illumines the night,
A shadow spreads.
Seeing the jewel in the lake,
You will gasp for breath.

Yoga-Shakti is his ornament
Whose seat is in Muladhara.
When He beckons,
She always moves up.
Having illuminated the Seven Floors,
Prabhu lights up in the secret room.

The stem of that lotus is open.
Filled with nectar,
It sways by itself.
On the red and white lake,
A pair of swans is swimming.
They make love
In the privacy
Of their jungle paradise.
Above is the City of Fire,
Incredibly hot;
Deceit and lies
Have no efficacy here.
Does talk beget riches?

By descending into the depths
Of the nether worlds,
Pick up the jewel
With the strength of your practices.
O Gopal, Gopal!

Take to your heart
This sweet song of Govindchand.
All Vedic arguments
Will dissolve away.
In the Living Death
You will see Him!

Song of Gopal

Commentary

The man of the Heart plays in the spiraling central channel of subtle energy, the Sushumna, which is tubelike. The five "elements" surrounding the ten-petaled lotus are earth, water, air, fire, and ether, corresponding respectively to the senses of smell, taste, touch, sight, and hearing. This verse suggests that those Adepts whose consciousness rises above the ten-petaled lotus enter a realm beyond the mundane senses, but that such a state is difficult to achieve.

The flower is the symbol of female sexual passion, and the fruit represents male sexual potency. At another level, the flower is the yoni and the fruit is the lingam. The phantasmagorical tree is the subtle body; its trunk is the spinal column. The creeper that "hangs ablaze" is the Shushumna, lit up by the Kundalini fire. The jewel in the lake (of passion) is an allegory of physical love, in which breath control is an aid to control over orgasm.

Yoga-Shakti refers to the Kundalini, whose abode is the Muladhara. The Seven Floors are seven ascending psychic centers (chakras); Prabhu is a name for the Immortal Soul and is also an epithet for the guru.

Swans represent sensual beings, graceful and discerning. The redness of the lake symbolizes menstrual blood and feminine energy; the whiteness, semen and masculine energy. The privacy of the swans' jungle paradise is at the sexual center, above which is the fiery realm at the navel (the solar plexus). Only those seekers who truly love without hypocrisy can pass through this psychic center of transformation.

The jewel of love rests in the depths of darkness; those who are able to retain the breath by yogic means can pick up this "jewel." Such ecstatics are beyond the injunctions of the Vedas; they "see" the Man when they abandon themselves to love and give up egotism. The song suggests that sexual yoga, when properly practiced, is the key to the direct experience of Divinity.

The Guru Bears the Fruits

How will you stand up effortlessly
If you do not find the Man of the Heart?

The roots of this tree are in the sky;
On the ground are its branches.
The tree has flowers but no fruits,
For the Guru bears the fruits in his hands.

The river Ganga dies of thirst;
The fire dies of cold.
The bird's nest is in the waters,
But the eggs rest on top of the tree.

In the North is his head;
In the South are his feet;
His hands are in the East;
From the West he speaks.

From three strings, a melody is created,
Producing the sound of music.
That music is like galloping hooves;
Be sure to keep the rhythm right.

The Guru will go in the boat;
I shall flow with the current.
We'll meet at the charnel ground
Beneath the neem tree.

Commentary

Since the sexual yoga of the Bauls emphasizes the feminine principle, here the yogic body is conceived as a woman's body, pictured as a tree with its roots in the crown of the head. The branches are the limbs of the body. The flowers are the center of energy, and the trunk is the spinal column. There are no fruits because this is the body of a woman, and fruits symbolize the male genitals. The Guru, who represents the highest state of consciousness, bears the essence, which is the causal principle of creation.

The river Ganga refers to the flow of menstrual fluid on the last day. It dies of thirst because after this period, the yoni is once again dry. Menstrual fluid, which has the nature of fire, "dies of cold" when its flow stops. The abode of the bird, the spirit of life, is on the "causal waters" where sexual play starts. Its created form, the egg, is on top of the tree, in the spiritual realm.

The Man of the Heart has his head in the skies and his feet on the ground. His actions are intuitive and his speech is clear.

The three strings are the three subtle channels of energy that flow through the spinal column. The music is the primordial vibration of cosmic energy.

The Guru goes in the vessel of love and devotion that has been built by the disciple. They meet on the funeral pyre of time, where they unite to become one.

The neem tree is said to cure all ills.

When Both Are United

If you want to catch Krishna,
First go and find a Shakti.

The Supreme Brahman
Is this same Krishna.
Man's wandering heart
Is the Uncatchable.

In Muladhara, the root lotus,
Is the cosmic Mother;
In Sahasrara, the head lotus,
The cosmic Father.
When both are united,
There is no more birth or death.

Will rituals and prayers
Bring about such union?
If so, why do yogis
Practice breath control constantly?

That which has been heard
From the Guru,
Is not to be spoken of;
Yet my heart cannot bear to wait.
"When, O Chandi Gosai,
Will you do your practices?"

Song of Chandi Gosai

Commentary

Those who wish to experience the love of Krishna must
assume the role of his lovers. Only those who arouse the
passionate longing of a woman can catch that elusive
experience of love. The cosmic Mother—or Kundalini, the
passionate energy—rests like a coiled snake in the root
lotus. She is awakened from her deep slumber by the
channeling of energies into the root lotus. Yogis do this
through breathing techniques. When she is awakened, she
uncoils and makes her way to the higher centers of
consciousness to unite with the cosmic Father. United, they
merge into an absolute state of nonduality.

The Blissful Enchantress

Oh, that beautiful blissful Yogini!
What ecstatic union must be Hers.
Many great yogis have become enraptured,
Seeing this Blissful Enchantress.

The Yogini's illusory power
Casts a shadow on the Universe.
One who recognizes this,
Understands that the Cosmic Union
Of Vrindaban
Is caused by the Eternal Play.

At the new moon She is at Triveni;
On the thirteenth day she is at Varuni.
In the form of the makara fish
She floats in the fast-flowing water.

Sitting at the lion-door,
She guards the entrance to the fort.
Colored water streams from Her eyes
As the snake spits out the jewel.

Says Ramarasa to Uttama:
"If you want to drink the nectar,
Go, place your heart at the lion-door!
You shall forever live in peace."

Song of Uttama

Commentary

Varuni is a place in Bengal by the holy river Ganga (the Ganges) where a festival is held on the thirteenth day of the waning moon in the month of Chaitra (around April). Women come from all over Bengal at that time to bathe in the purifying waters of the Ganges. Esoterically, Varuni is a term for the restless sexual energy.

The makara fish is a mythical crocodile-like creature that carried the goddess Ganga on its back, from the mountains to the sea. The lion-door is the main entrance to the house of ecstasy; this is the yoni, where the man places his lingam, the head of the snake.

The Three-Cornered Lake

O Spirit of a Baul,
Where will you go,
Leaving behind this worldly existence?

O Baul,
There is a three-cornered lake
Where many colorful birds abide.
When the bird leaves through the throat,
Flies come to the mouth.

O Baul,
The lightning is born in water;
Creepers entwine with leaves.
Where did you cook your food
When you were in your mother's womb?

O Baul,
The deer's home
Is on the lion's head,
Where the peacocks abide.
Your head will surely fall
When the two peacocks fly away.

O Baul,
Do not take lightly
This saying of Gosain Uttamchand.
Now that the body is taking a golden hue,
Its jewels are being robbed.

O Baul,
Do not put your radish
Into another's wealth,
Into another's woman.
Cross the sea of existence effortlessly.
Where is your home, O Baul?

Song of Gosain Uttamchand

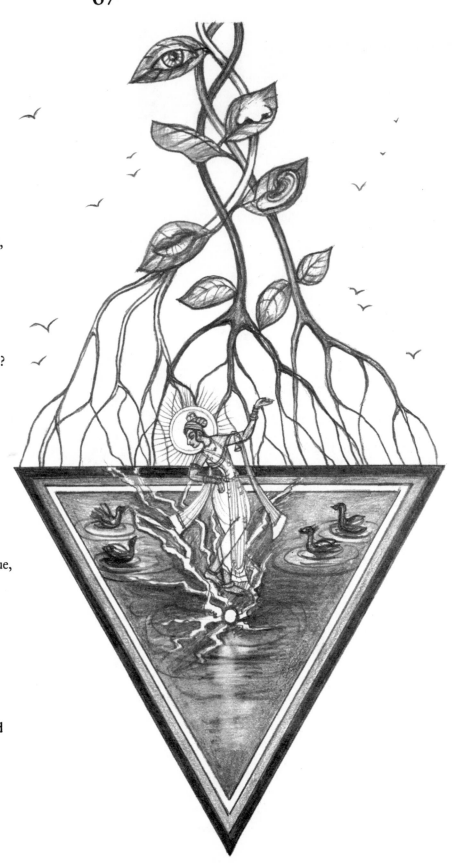

Commentary

Bauls do not believe in searching for a spiritual goal outside themselves. Worldly existence cannot be denied so long as the body lives. The "three-cornered lake" refers to the yoni within, the region of sexual passion where many fantasies abide. The lightning is the fleeting Man of the Heart, who manifests himself in the "causal waters." The creepers represent the subtle channels of energy and the leaves are symbols of the organs of sense perception.

The deer is a symbol of Krishna, who rests at the highest center of consciousness in the crown of the head. The lion is the yogic body as a female, in the guise of Radha, the passionate lover. The peacocks are the divine lovers in their transcendental aspect. When the divine spirit leaves the body, there is death. The radish is a colloquial term for the lingam. "Another's woman" refers to the physical body of a woman. One's own woman is the "woman within." The ultimate spiritual union is of the male and female within. Bauls search for their spiritual nourishment within the microcosm.

The Chand-Chakora Birds

Enclosed by moonbeams
A million miles apart,
The chand-chakora birds
Fly about.

If you could know
How those birds unite,
Month after month
At the moon's transition,
Your practices
Would be complete.

There is a mysterious saying:
"Frogs eat the snake's head."
Hearing of the frog's courage,
I am amazed.

Of that Sensual Enchantress,
I have heard from Lalan's lips.
On singing this song, Duddu asks:
"How can I catch the moon?"

Song of Duddu

Commentary

The chand-chakoras are mythical birds that are said to sustain
themselves on moonbeam nectar. They symbolize the sensual
adepts who are able to sustain themselves on the fruits of their
yogic endeavors. The union of the birds at the moon's transition
refers to the Bauls' sexual rites practiced at the time of
menstruation. This sexual rite is called "raising the full moon
at new moon time." On completion of the rite, the inner light
illuminates the darkness of ignorance.

The frog symbolizes the yoni, and the snake is the lingam.

The Jailhouse of Love

Trouble has struck the Jailhouse of Love;
The Thief of Love has been caught
In the clutches of the Sensual One.
He has been caught by placing snares
In the path of the Vital Wind.

For two full days the thief remains
In the custody of the faith-police.
On the third day,
All tied up and bound,
He is sent for trial.

The sadhaka comes to know
That the theif rests
In the Eternal Abode.
Says Lalan:
"This vision comes
With the dawning of Divine Knowledge."

Song of Lalan

Commentary

The Thief of Love is Krishna, the Uncatchable Man, who causes pandemonium in the "Jailhouse of Love," the physical body of a woman. This refers to the menstrual period, when the masculine element, the divine image, manifests itself in the woman's body. The snare with which to catch the divine image, the symbol of pure love, is the aperture at the back of the throat that connects the throat with the nasal passages. Bauls believe that by closing this aperture through yogic means, one achieves liberation and immortality.

The Thief of Love hides in the menstrual fluid for two days and then becomes manifest on the third day. The spiritual disciple, or sadhaka, who "catches" this Thief realizes that he is none other than Krishna, whose paradise is the Eternal Abode.

The Inner Moon

The full moon is veiled by clouds;
Until the clouds move away,
The moon will not be visible.

When your clouds move away,
The Inner Moon will appear.
You will see in this Moon of
    Wisdom
The light of a million moons.

In the cloud's lap
The moon rests;
In the moon's lap
Is its lover, the lightning.

Of revealing the moon
By dispelling the clouds,
Much has been written.

In darkness, Madan cries:
"I am alone and confused!"
One who has the Guru's grace,
Gets to see the Moon!

                    Song of Madan

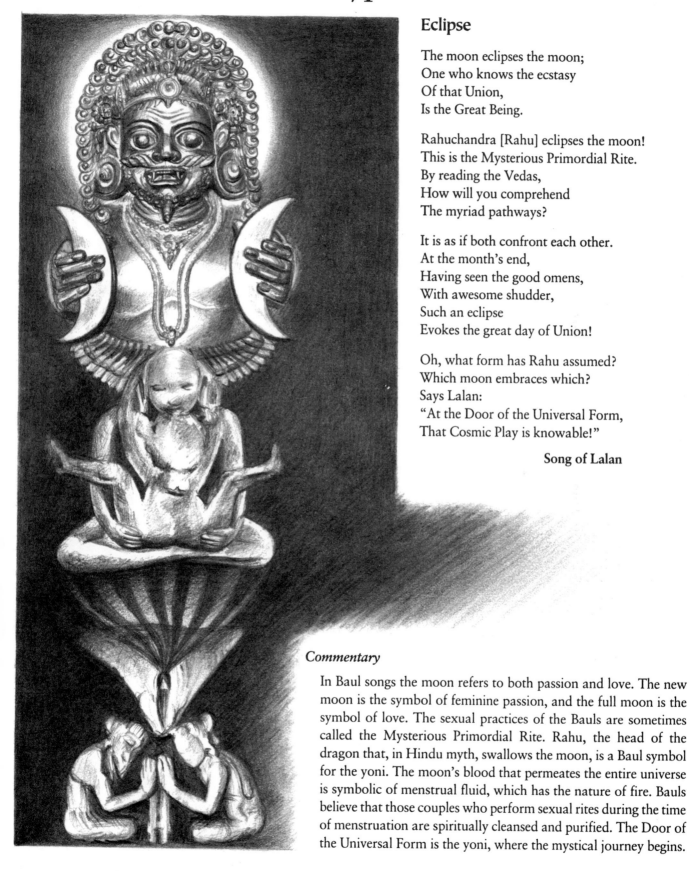

Eclipse

The moon eclipses the moon;
One who knows the ecstasy
Of that Union,
Is the Great Being.

Rahuchandra [Rahu] eclipses the moon!
This is the Mysterious Primordial Rite.
By reading the Vedas,
How will you comprehend
The myriad pathways?

It is as if both confront each other.
At the month's end,
Having seen the good omens,
With awesome shudder,
Such an eclipse
Evokes the great day of Union!

Oh, what form has Rahu assumed?
Which moon embraces which?
Says Lalan:
"At the Door of the Universal Form,
That Cosmic Play is knowable!"

Song of Lalan

Commentary

In Baul songs the moon refers to both passion and love. The new moon is the symbol of feminine passion, and the full moon is the symbol of love. The sexual practices of the Bauls are sometimes called the Mysterious Primordial Rite. Rahu, the head of the dragon that, in Hindu myth, swallows the moon, is a Baul symbol for the yoni. The moon's blood that permeates the entire universe is symbolic of menstrual fluid, which has the nature of fire. Bauls believe that those couples who perform sexual rites during the time of menstruation are spiritually cleansed and purified. The Door of the Universal Form is the yoni, where the mystical journey begins.

That Flower

That flower can be found
In the gardener's garden.
Who but my Guru
Would know of it?

On the day when the full moon
And the new moon unite,
The bee does not go
With his scorched Shakti
To that flower
Whose perfume is eternal.

Its stalk is inverted;
It is six-petaled,
With stamens at the center.
Unfortunately for the gods,
On that day,
Even the brahmins
Cannot have their satisfaction!

To whom will you give the flower
When you have plucked it?
Who knows the mantra
For its worship?
O mad one!
Wandering about,
Trying to pick the flower,
How will you be able
To find your way back?

Says Mad Rejo:
"One who wishes to pick that flower,
Upon receiving initiation,
Should put on a renunciate's loincloth."

Song of Rejo Khepa

Commentary

The "gardener's garden" is the divine body as a woman. She is the gardener and the guru; she alone knows the mysterious blossoming of her passion.

For most Hindus, intercourse during menstruation is taboo. The bee symbolizes the man; his "scorched Shakti" is the menstruating woman.

The six-petaled lotus, the sexual center, has an inverted stalk with its roots in the void. Those who wish to "pick" this flower must be prepared to go through the labyrinth of emotions. Only true renunciates can bear the ordeal, for having surrendered to the Divine Will, they have no expectations or goals to achieve.

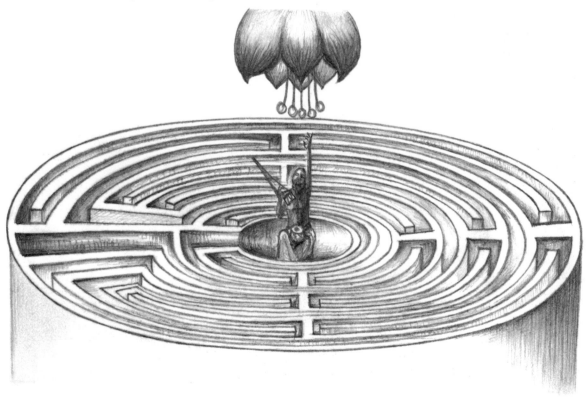

You Will See the Light

Where is the moon's abode?
Into which whirlpool does the night swirl?
Whence does it issue?

Everyone knows
Of the eclipse at full moon;
How many can see
The eclipse at new moon?
Understand, O mind,
The rites of the four moons.
In observing them
All suffering of the mortal body
Will be overcome.

Observe the waxing and waning
Of the moon;
Only then will your radiant full moon arise.
The two moons, becoming one,
Complete the Union.
The half moon is the Secret Woman
Whose husband resides
At the Root of Creation.

One who manifests the full moon
At the time of the new moon,
Spreads joy throughout the three worlds.
This rite is not for ordinary beings;
On completion of it,
One becomes immortal.
Gosai Ramlal says:
"O Gopal! You will see the Light!"

Song of Gopal

Commentary

In the phenomenal world, the lunar eclipse takes place during the full moon—but what of the world within? The eclipse at new moon refers to the menstrual period when Bauls practice their sexual rites.

The "half moon" is the period after the three "days" of menstruation when the last traces of the flow ebb away.

Rites of Love

He does not know the rites of love.
Can mere talk sustain Love?

The rites of love
Have been expounded by our Guru.
If you want to make love,
Go, touch the feet of a holy man.

Having completed the three stages of initiation,
One finds the Jewel of Love.
Having learned the Art of Archery,
Go, show your bravery in battle.
If you fight without arrows,
Your downfall will be immediate.

Aren't people dumb?
They only speak to talk;
Sleeping on a torn mat,
They dream of becoming millionaires.

Inside a cow is her urine,
Yet she does not know its worth.
There is a jewel on the snake's head,
But it eats like a beggar.

Song of Padmalochan

Commentary

The Bauls believe that love must be cultivated and nurtured with tenderness and devoted effort. Those who go through the three stages of initiation find the treasures on completing their spiritual discipline. The Art of Archery is the yogic practice whereby sexual passion is transformed into a divine experience. Hindus consider the cow sacred and its urine a sacrament. Traditional Indian medicine also regards urine as an antiseptic.

For an explanation of the jewel on the snake's head, see commentary on song 49. The song points out that, though the snake has a jewel, it still eats only vermin.

Those Who Worship the Moon

This is the way of the fakirs
Who do not follow the scriptures.
They do not follow the Koran
Without the guru's instructions.

Having received the "word" from the guru,
They worship the sun and the moon.
Those who worship the moon
Practice the discipline of the five rasas.
By observing the three moons,
They drink the mixture of rasa and bija.

Their hair is in matted locks;
They drink a lot of bhang
And smoke heaps of ganja.
They talk in riddles
So difficult to understand!

People are moved upon hearing them
Sing their enchanting songs.
Says humble Rasik:
These Auls, Bauls, and Bald Heads are so
   contrary.

Commentary

The sun and the moon refer to the solar and lunar energies within the body. They also represent the powers of passion and love. Rasa, in this context, refers to ova, and bija to semen. Bhang is a drink made from ground marijuana leaves, and ganja is the flowering tops that are smoked. Auls and Bauls are subsects within the Baul cult, and Bald Heads are the Fakirs, or Muslim mendicants.

76

Mistaking Poison for Nectar

If you don't know the taste of rasa
Your sadhana will be futile
By mistaking poison for nectar,
You will die in pain.

The rasa in which the Guru resides
Has many distinctive qualities;
O mad mind, it is very subtle!
One who tastes the rasa,
Knowing the various qualities,
Is truly a Sensual One.

The Guru hides secretly
In the nectar-rasa.
On the second day of the dark moon
The lotus blooms.

One who forgets that yoga
And forsakes the Union
Brings bad luck upon himself.
Says Panja:
"In all this chaos
I have forgotten my sadhana."

Song of Panja Saha

Commentary

In this song rasa refers to the erotic mood as a divine sentiment. Sexual passion can be either transformed into a spiritual experience or debased into lust.

The Guru is rati, the essence of love, which hides in the rasa, the divine sentiment. Bauls attempt to catch this sentiment by means of sexual rites performed during the woman's menstruation. The period of the first flow of menstruation is known as the new (or dark) moon. The second period is known as the "first day," and the third and final period is known as the "second day." The "nectar-rasa" flows on the final day.

To Catch the Snake

First learn the mantra
With which to catch the snake.
Then, with prayer beads around your neck,
Go into the overgrown forest.

The snake guards the treasure
Beneath the floor of the house;
Six mice have tunneled
Right through the foundations.

The frog dances near the snake;
The snake slithers beneath the treasure.
Having become the Master,
The frog cannot be caught.

If one consecrates turmeric paste
With the mantra,
Then the snake will be subdued
Upon smelling it.
Says Abdullah:
"I lie beneath the feet
Of the Precious Teacher."

Song of Abdullah

Commentary

In this song, the snake is a dual symbol. In the first instance it symbolizes passion. Abdullah suggests that those who wish to experience sexual passion through the body of woman should first receive initiation and then practice spiritual discipline and yogic techniques before embarking on the sexual practices. The wealth of spiritual experience lies behind passion. The six mice represent the six delusions (anger, pride, envy, greed, lust, and avarice).

In the second instance, the snake represents the lingam, and the frog is the yoni. The guru-principle is considered feminine during the stage when sexual yoga is practiced.

The turmeric paste (*vivek-haldi*) refers to feces, one of the four sacraments that are used during Baul sexual rites. It is a symbol of discerning wisdom, by which one can distinguish between lust and love.

That Emotion

First try to discover the emotions.
Having embraced them and made love,
You will find the Jewel of Love.
The Effortless Man resides in that emotion
Which arises just before dark.

That emotion which is beyond the realm of the senses
Is difficult to experience without a guru.
The scriptures say that its qualities are eternal;
Unable to recognize it,
Mortals roam in the eighty-four realms.

Catching the flow of that emotion,
He is carried away on a river of milk.
Thus the Effortless Man comes
And plays in that emotion.
Even one drop of that emotion
Vanquishes death immediately.

"New moon" is the name of this special
    Union.
On the first day of the waxing moon,
There are no duties to be performed;
It is on the second day
That the spiritual rites take place.
Says Panja:
"I worship the feet of one
Who can mix milk and water
In the vessel within."

Song of Panja Saha

Commentary

The jewel of Love floats in the raging waters of passion. The Effortless Man is that "jewel" of erotic sentiment that becomes the object of love. The "emotion which arises just before dark" refers to the fifth rasa, known as Madhurya. Bauls believe that it is possible to commune with the Divine only when one accepts the object of worship as a lover. This experience is beyond the mundane reality of worldly life (symbolized by the eighty-four realms).

The term "emotion" in this song also refers to the sexual rites of the Bauls during the menstruation of the woman. "New Moon" refers to the menstrual flow on the first day. It is only on the third day, which is called the "second day," that Bauls attempt to catch the Effortless Man.

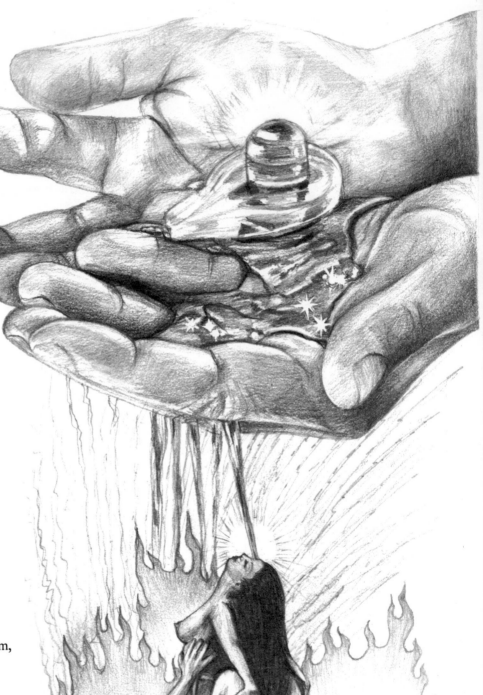

That Powerful Rite

That powerful rite
Is difficult to perform.
Only a sensuous one can know
The secret of the fluids
And the greatness of that Union.

Having closed the snake's mouth
With his hand,
The sensual one sits without fear.
Having drunk poison,
He tastes nectar,
And so experiences
The Living Death.

Having seen the form within the form,
He holds up the mirror of emotion.
Having cooled the fire,
He as places quicksilver on it.

Says Gosai Guruchand:
O mind!
Stay submerged in the ocean waters.
When the water
Turns to quicksilver,
Sink the boat on dry land!

Song of Gosai Guruchand

Commentary

The Bauls believe that one should embark on sexual practices only when one has become discerning. The truly "sensual ones" are those who can distinguish intuitively between good and bad, love and lust. The "secret of the fluids" refers to the invigorating power of sexual secretions, either externally or internally, by acts of conscious retention. "Closing the snake's mouth" refers to a sexual-yogic technique of applying pressure to the base of the lingam with the hand, in order to prevent ejaculation.

The "form within the form" is an enigmatic phrase whose meaning hides behind the play of words. The first form is the Man of the Heart, and the second form is the menstrual fluid. The Baul yogi who is able to catch the Man is bestowed with a nectar-like grace, symbolized by quicksilver, which cools and consumes the fire of passion. Quicksilver also refers to the masculine sexual energy in its most subtle and transformed aspect as Divine Love. When passion, symbolized by water, is transformed into Divine Love, the yogi returns to the world of physicality, to participate once more in the ecstasies of everyday life.

The Three Rivers

The Uncatchable Man has moored himself
At the banks of the river;
Having crystallized the Jewels of Love,
He has weighed anchor.

The two sister rivers meet
In the salty waters of the Ganges.
The ebbing tide plays in three forms,
In the waters of the three rivers.

The Primordial Man has caught three forms
In the Uncatchable Moon;
He plays in the three streams,
Blending himself with the three flavors.

The Man, becoming three women,
Rides the waves of the three fluids.
He assumes a threefold nature:
Worldly, celestial, and divine.

As poison, She is worldly;
As the essence of beauty, She is celestial;
As the taste of nectar, She is divine.

Only one who is sensual
Can prepare the nectar.
One who has the Guru's grace
Can go to the river
To play with the three women.

The nymphs bestow their grace
When the sexual fluids are controlled.
At the Third Eye,
One has the Living Death.
Sitting by the river banks,
It is easy to catch the Man.

Song of Panja Saha

Commentary

The most important sexual rite of the Bauls takes place during the menstruation of the woman. It is at this time that the Bauls endeavor to catch the Uncatchable Man. This divine form in woman, the perfect creative masculine image, normally plays at the two-petaled lotus, the Third Eye; but during menstruation the Man comes down to the sexual center. The banks of the river represent the yoni.

During the first stage of menstruation, the fluid that is emitted is dark in color. This is first of the three "rivers" and is called Yamuna; it has the attribute of inertia (*tamas*). During the second stage, the fluid is red and the river is called Saraswati; it has the attribute of activity and passion (*rajas*). The salty water of the Ganges that flows on the third day is white in color and has the attribute of revelation (*sattva*). Each of these different "rivers" has a distinct flavor linked to a sentiment.

The primordial Man is the Uncatchable Man who assumes three forms during the three states of menstruation. These are the three expressions of masculine attitude. The woman who emits "poison" fluid on the first day is selfish and craves pleasure only for herself. The man who experiences the desire of such passion is worldly and seeks only self-gratification. On the second day, the nature of the woman is celestial; she seeks as well as gives pleasure. The man who unites with this heavenly nymph experiences supranatural reality, a magical world where gods play. Erotic passion as a divine sentiment is the nature of the woman on the third day, and its corresponding masculine experience is that of selfish love.

The song proceeds to point out that one must become an adept of sexual yoga in order to experience the supreme moment of cosmic orgasm (the "living death").

The Three Girls

Occasionally the three rivers,
Ganga, Yamuna, and Saraswati,
Flood down together at Triveni.

The rivers swell up
When the three girls play.
One is dark,
One is fair,
One is red like a ruby.

How many know of the virtues
These three girls possess?
Only Shiva can tell!
Pashupati, Lord of Beasts,
Catches one in his locks
And one on his chest.

The Sensual Girl stays at home.
She sees the world
In the spirit of her house.
Her witness is the cowherder's daughter,
Krishna's Beloved One.
Being chaste, she upholds the Dharma.

This time, when I die,
I want to be reborn as a woman.
I'll request the company
Of great souls.
Says Das Kangal:
"I won't have to keep my lineage
alight!"

Song of Kangal

Commentary

For an explanation of the symbolism of the three rivers, see the commentary on song 80. The colors of the "three girls" refer to the different colors of menstrual blood during the initial "three days" of menstruation.

Shiva, the Supreme Yogi, is also called Pashupati, Lord of Beasts, because he has conquered his animal passions and wild instincts. He catches the flow of the first two "rivers" on his outward body, and the third he catches within his inner being. This symbolizes the benefits, both physical and spiritual, that are attainable through correct practice of the three-day rite.

The Sensual Girl who stays at home is Radha, who sees her Beloved within herself. Though Radha was married to another man, she is still considered chaste because in her love for Krishna she was unhypocritical and ultimately true to her highest sentiments.

Kangal wishes to be reborn as a woman so that he can experience the love of Krishna. He also refers to the patriarchal Bengali society, in which men have the responsibility of maintaining their family tradition, thus getting bound to worldly pursuits.

The River of Passion

Dive not into the river of passion;
You won't find its shores.
That vast river's current is strong;
It has no banks.

Don't dive in!
Stay on the side
And watch out for the tides.
By anointing the body
With the paste of discernment,
The crocodile can do no harm.

What competency do you have,
That you attempt to swim across?
Only try to do it
If the Guru offers support.

Those who are masters
Of the five rasas
Know the play of the tides;
Their boats do not sink.
Paddled by the oars of Love
They row onward.

When milk and water
Are mixed together,
The water alone flows upstream.
Says Dvija Kailashchandra:
"The swan swims in this special way."

Song of Dvija Kailashchandra

Commentary

The crocodile of passion lurks in the dangerous waters of sexuality. The paste of discernment (*vivek-haldi*) is feces, one of the four sacraments used ritualistically during the Bauls' sexual practices. Those who are masters of the five rasas, or devotional sentiments, are able to float on the raging waters of emotion. Milk is the symbol of love, and water represents erotic passion. Swans are sensual beings who are able to distinguish between the two (see commentary on song 49). The term *Panamahansa*, or "great swan," is customarily used to honor great yogis.

Where the Three Rivers Meet

How are you going to cross that place
Where the three rivers meet?
Deceitful sadhus are dying at its shores!

Three Attributes form Triveni;
The three Shaktis reside there.
They manifest on the day of Union,
For the Liberation of all beings.
One who has faith in the Way of
    Woman
Is ferried across by the Great Mother.

At the time of the full moon at new
    moon,
The current gets stronger
With the approaching floods.
Large chains of waves
Rise up to the banks.
On that day, the crocodile of passion
Is in great anguish;
It eats all those
Who fall into the water!

Accomplished yogis go to the banks;
Seeing the rivers flowing,
They lose themselves in bliss.
Some are able to cross
By the strength of their practices,
While others drown.

Three rivers combine
Into a threefold knot.
The Tent of the Head
Is both upside down and inside out.
Says Chandi Gosai:
"Sacrifice your self at midnight!"

Song of Chandi Gosai

Commentary

The Bauls' sexual rites during menstruation are known as "the full moon at new moon." The full moon symbolizes the revelatory nature of love, and the new moon is a symbol of the mysterious nature of passion. During this time passion floods down to the sexual region of the woman. The "crocodile of passion" represents the deluding power of sexual energy; at a more esoteric level, it is a symbol of the act of breath retention. Those who cross the river that separates the outer world and the inner world by holding their breath are able to avoid the clutches of the crocodile. Only the true *Sadhus,* or holy men, are able to cross these dangerous waters. They have renounced the ego and surrendered to the grace and light of faith. The "Tent of the Head" is the thousand-petaled lotus. Midnight is a time that Tantrics believe is charged with potency.

The Living Death

The Man of Breath
Moves by breath alone;
The Peaceful Man
Rests on peace;
A third Man
Hides in secrecy.
Practice your Sadhana
Knowing this.

Of the three Men,
Which one will you seek?
There are three ways
To find them.
But first find the Guru, O mind!

There is the Door of Birth,
And the Door of Death.
But to whom shall I speak
Of the other Door?
One who is born
At the Door of Death
Becomes immortal.

The three Men reside
In the three fluids
For three days.
For half a day,
Mother Nature secretly waits.
Says Gosai Ramlal to Gopal:
"Before you die,
Be sure to have a Living Death!"

Song of Gopal

Commentary

The Man of Breath is the worldly man who lives only so long as he breathes. The Man of Peace is one who, because of virtuous deeds, enjoys the delights of heaven. He is content only until the fruits of his good deeds run dry; then he returns to earthly existence. The Man who hides in secrecy is the Man of the Heart, the immortal light of existence. To experience him, one must be reborn after the death of one's ego through surrender and renunciation.

The Man of Breath comes down with the first flow of the menstrual fluid; the Peaceful Man comes during the second flow; and the Man of the Heart descends on the final day. The half-day is the period after the third flow when the menstrual fluids start to ebb. This when the Bauls employ their yoga to catch the Hidden Man.

Part Three

◆

THE WAY OF LOVE

THE TRUTH WITHIN
THE BODY

The central concept of Baul philosophy and practice is *Deha-Tattva,* the "Truth within the Body." The Bauls regard the human body as a microcosm, a small scale replica of the greater universe, in which all the elements of existence reside. While the body's outward nature is transient, its innermost essence is eternal. The body is both the experience and the field of experience, the worshiper and the shrine. In such a philosophy, even basic physical functions take on a cosmic significance, for it is from the earthly reality of the body that the inward spiritual journey begins. From this gross material plane of existence, consciousness slowly ascends through the various subtle planes of experience finally to reach the ultimate state of Absolute Unity. In the words of the Bauls, "one plunges deep within to soar beyond."

The Absolute state of nonduality is achieved through the union of Shiva and Shakti, the two cosmic principles that represent the basic duality of the microcosm. Shiva is the static and objective masculine aspect, the luminous ideal, changeless and eternal. Shakti, his feminine counterpart, is the dynamic and subjective aspect; by her power she creates the myriad forms within the universe.

Thus body is a universe, a womb within which all forms are created and evolved. Only the bearer of this womb knows its mysteries; only a woman truly knows the experience of conception, gestation, and birth.

> *I hear that Mother Nature,*
> *Seeing the Indivisible Spirit,*
> *Created the universe*
> *From within herself.*
> *That is why it is said:*
> *"Within the universe*
> *All have the nature of woman,*
> *Not man."*
>
> *song 37*

This, in the words of the Bauls, "To find the Man of the Heart, one must first become a woman." This refers not only to male but also to female aspirants, who must also learn to awaken the dormant feminine energy within both body and mind.

The Bauls borrowed their vision of the microcosm from the Sahajiya Tantrics, who taught that this dynamic energy flows through numerous subtle channels that permeate the body. The three most important channels are within the spinal cord: *Ida,* on the left; *Pingala,* on the right; and *Shushumna,* in the center. Ida has the nature of the moon; through this channel flow the emotional, intuitive, and reflective energies. Through Pingala, symbolized by the sun, flow the intellectual, analytical, and expressive energies. In the central Shushumna, the "fire of time" consumes and transforms the experiences of duality. Emotion and intellect, intuition and analysis, reflection and expression all lose their dichotomy and become a flow of pure ecstatic energy.

Running from the base of the spine to the cortex of the brain, these three subtle channels are "knotted" together at each end. At these two ends and at various points in between, the Ida and Pingala are pictured as forming bow-like shapes around the subtle centers of energy located along the central Shushumna. These energy centers, called *chakras,* represent ascending stages of consciousness. Consciousness becomes manifest in gross or worldly levels at the lowest chakra and proceeds through the various subtle levels to the highest chakra, where transcendental consciousness is manifest.

In some Tantric schools, the chakra system has been highly codified, almost to the point of rigidity. The Bauls, however, have not adopted any definite system, perhaps because of their nonintellectual approach and their anarchic mystical disposition. In actual yogic practice, outer descriptions are superfluous, because one deals with what *is,* not with what is "supposed to be." In their songs, however, the Bauls do refer to the various yogic experiences and concepts—not in order to describe or define them but rather to suggest or evoke impressions of them by poetic means.

Bauls usually sing of four main chakras in which the biological, psychological, spiritual, and cosmic forces interact and play. The fifth chakra is the transcendental realm, beyond the duality of the microcosm. The chakras are poetically visualized as lotuses with varying numbers of petals.

The root center, which lies at the bottom of the spine, is the *Muladhara* chakra, the four-petaled lotus. It has the nature of earth, of physical reality. Here Kundalini, the latent power of Shakti, lies dormant, like a coiled serpent. When she is awakened by the power of passion, she uncoils and releases her energy, which travels up the central channel, the Shushumna. Her

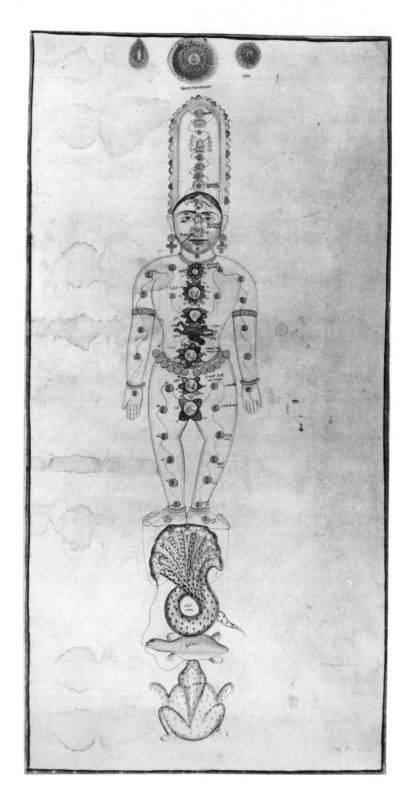

The subtle body, depicted in a nineteenth-century painting from northeast India. Photo by Nik Douglas.

destination is the *Ajna* chakra, the "Third Eye," visualized as a two-petaled lotus. There she unites with the Man of the Heart. He is referred to as Ishwara (another name for Shiva), the Lord of all beings, and she is Adyashakti, the primordial power.

During sexual union, the couple's physical convergence takes place just above the root lotus, while their spirituality blends together at the two-petaled lotus. In Vaishnava terms, this is where Radha and Krishna unite and enter as one into the eternal realm called Goloka, Krishna's paradise.

> *Full of light is this Eternal Realm*
> *In which the whole of Creation resides.*
> *Having reached the two-petaled lotus,*
> *Everything becomes known;*
> *No obstacles remain.*
>
> song 59

The three subtle channels of energy emerge out of the "knot" at the Muladhara or root lotus and rejoin at the Ajna or two-petaled lotus.

The three channels are symbolized by the three holy rivers of the Hindus: Ganga (Ganges), Yamuna, and Saraswati. Ganga is Ida, the lunar channel; Yamuna is Pingala, the solar channel; and Saraswati is Shushumna, the fiery one. In India, the confluence of the three rivers (near Allahabad in the North) is called Triveni. Thus, Triveni is also the term for the confluences of the subtle channels at the Muladhara and Ajna chakras.

The Tantric tradition speaks of several centers between the root lotus and the two-petaled lotus, but according to the Bauls only two of them are important: the *Sadadal,* or six-petaled lotus, and the *Manipura,* or ten-petaled lotus.

The six-petaled Sadadal lotus is above the four-petaled root lotus. Here the sexual energies become manifest. The six-petaled lotus is described as floating on the primeval or "causal" waters, which are the source of life. The physical manifestations of the energy of the Sadadal chakra are semen and ova. This chakra is the realm of rasa, the undifferentiated and restless ocean of passion. From the banks of this vast ocean, Radha calls to her beloved Krishna to ferry her across the waters of Existence.

> *If you have come*
> *With the boat of your sacred name,*
> *O Hari,*
> *Then take me across!*
>
> song 24

To cross this ocean of Existence, the aspirant must surrender the ego, conquer delusions, and pass through the purifying fire of spirituality.

Above the six-petaled lotus is the ten-petaled Manipura, the "Jewel City." In the physical body, this chakra coincides with the place of digestion. In the metabolic breakdown of the food we eat, the good and useful are assimilated and the poisons are eliminated. In spiritual terms, this chakra is where the fire within the microcosm burns away all impurities, so that only Truth remains. Only those yogis who have transcended the realm of the senses are pure enough to withstand this "ordeal of fire."

> *The Man is playing*
> *In the spiraling tube.*
> *The five elements*
> *Surrounding the ten-petaled lotus*
> *Are tough indeed!*
>
> song 63

As the Kundalini energy rises, layers of consciousness unfold and the lotuses turn inward. Rasa, the restless sexual passion, is transformed into *rati,* the calm, restful experience of transcendental Love.

The Bauls also visualize the six-petaled lotus as floating on the causal waters; in the depths below is a "hundred-petaled lotus." Like a pearl-diver, the aspirant retains his breath (a reference to yogic practice), dives deep into the "ocean of rasa," and retrieves the jewel that rests deep within.

Above the causal waters, where a raging fire burns, is a ten-petaled lotus; above that is a two-petaled one. The thousand-petaled lotus rests in a place beyond time and space.

In another vivid symbol that the Bauls borrowed from Tantrism, the human body is visualized as an inverted tree with its roots in the thousand-petaled lotus (the crown or head chakra). The tree hangs over the causal waters, on which a six-petaled lotus floats. The trunk of the tree symbolizes the spinal column, and the branches are the limbs of the body. The milky fruit that hangs above the floating lotus is the Man of the Heart. The floating lotus is a symbol of the yoni (since it is the six-petaled lotus, the chakra in which the sexual energies are manifest), containing the "honey of passion." When the lotus embraces the Man of the Heart, ambrosia is formed by the honey mixing with the milky juice of the fruit. This sexual symbolism is typical of the Baul songs.

Objects of nature are not the only symbols that the Bauls use to illustrate Deha-Tattva. They also use items of everyday life to symbolize and illustrate their beliefs. The body is sometimes seen as an earthen pot filled with rasa, or as a bird cage, a train, or a bicycle. No matter what metaphor is employed, the concept of Truth within the Body is always present.

Rasa: The Juice of Love

Rasa literally means "fluids" or "juice." It is associated with taste and flavor. In Hindu medicine and science, *rasa* is the general term for bodily fluids or chemicals. The ancient Hindu school of alchemy, *rasayana,* sought to transform rasa by yogic means, from gross to subtle, from material to spiritual.

For the Bauls, *rasa* is a broad term used to denote not only bodily fluids such as semen and menstrual fluid, but also emotional experiences and microcosmic principles. As a symbol of the dynamic sexual energy, rasa is often likened to a liquid that, while simmering over a slow fire, steadily becomes thicker and more concentrated.

> *Keeping the mind steady,*
> *Stir the rasa,*
> *So achieving transformation.*
>
> *Watch carefully.*
> *Passion makes the rasa*
> *Go round and round.*
> *From passion comes*
> *The seed of love.*
>
> song 31

Passion gradually evolves toward the all-embracing experience of love: Radha's longing brings her to union with her beloved Krishna.

> *Does everyone know of that emotion*
> *Which binds Krishna to the Gopis?*
> *Only bees, with pure rasa,*
> *Know the love of the Gopis.*
>
> song 32

One tastes this emotion, sometimes conceived as sweet and sticky honey, and relishes it, just as one enjoys the passion of a kiss.

> One who tastes the rasa,
> Knowing the various qualities,
> Is truly a Sensual One.
>
> **song 76**

In the ultimate experience, there is no distinction between the taster, the tasted, and the taste—just as in the sacred union of Radha and Krishna there is no distinction between the lover, the beloved, and the love itself.

The Five Rasas

Rasa also refers to a devotional sentiment that reflects the devotee's love for Krishna, *Krishna-rati*. According to the Bauls, there are five dominant sentiments in an ascending order of intensity, indicating the closeness of the devotee's relationship with Krishna. Each sentiment is aroused by a particular type of stimulus.

The first sentiment is *Shanta,* meaning "peaceful." It is the quiet stage of devotion when the mind fixes itself on the object of worship. The heart and mind must be calm before one can embark on the whirlwind journey of passion. This sentiment is stimulated by listening to the guru's teachings, learning the basics of yoga, and keeping the company of good people.

The second sentiment is *Dasya*. In this stage the devotee worships Krishna as master and offers Him all the fruit of his works. The devotee seeks to overcome the six delusions: pride, greed, lust, envy, anger, and avarice. The guru encourages the disciple at this stage by bestowing love and grace.

The third sentiment is *Sakhya*. Here Krishna is seen as a friend. The Baul bases his relationship with Krishna on loyalty and faith; they have no secrets from each other. The devotee conditions himself into this state first by seeing Krishna as his friend and then by recognizing his friends as Krishna. He is further stimulated by the joy experienced in the innocent playfulness of friendship.

The fourth sentiment is *Vatsalya*. Now Krishna is loved as one's child.

The legends tell of Krishna as a naughty, mischievous child who nevertheless was always forgiven and tenderly loved by his parents. This compassionate and selfless attitude is stimulated by enjoying the company of children, loving them through all their moods and pranks, and recognizing childlike innocence as an attribute of Krishna.

The fifth sentiment is *Madhurya*. In this final state, the devotee regards Krishna as a lover. For many Bauls, the previous four sentiments are virtually insignificant in comparison with this one; they regard Madhurya as the fundamental sentiment, the rasa out of which all other rasas flow. Those who are able to crystallize this erotic sentiment find the Jewel Man.

> *Those who are masters*
> *Of the five rasas*
> *Know the play of the tides.*
> *Their boats do not sink.*
> *Paddled by the oars of Love,*
> *They row onward.*
>   **song 82**

Erotic passion is the feeling produced from "floating" in the Madhurya rasa. This is the condition of Radha and the Gopis, who forsook all other sentiments in order to experience the passionate ecstasy of Krishna's Being.

> *That youthful, sensual, ecstatic maiden*
> *Gives such sweet honey;*
> *Krishna Himself appears!*
>   **song 41**

The Path of Passionate Devotion

In Vaishnavism there are two distinct types of devotion: *vaidhi* and *raganuga*. Vaidhi is the more intellectual approach, the path of those who perform rituals and observe the prescribed religious duties. These worshipers base their practice on intellectual conviction and belief in the majesty and omnipotence of the Divine. Through performing religious duties, they hope to acquire merits by which they can gradually approach their goal. Through vaidhi one gains entry into the celestial regions after death; happiness and contentment are the rewards of this type of devotion.

In contrast, raganuga is an emotional path. The word *raga* implies a mood or emotion spontaneously evoked by an object of desire. Thus, to follow raganuga is to follow the natural inclinations of the heart. This is the way of the Bauls, who seek not merely contentment but intense divine ecstasy. To achieve this, the devotee must be consumed with passionate longing to become one with the object of worship—like the intense yearning of Radha for union with Krishna. The lover must be willing to abandon the limited self and surrender unconditionally to the divine Beloved.

In raganuga, love is both the means and the end of the spiritual quest, both the path and the goal. Those whose devotion springs directly from the heart have no need for the medium of ritualistic observance. Through the power of love they commune with the divinity within.

> *They do no work*
> *That has no love.*
> *All orthodox rules of conduct*
> *Are left behind.*
>
> *They only acknowledge the way*
> *Of the Sensual King of Emotions.*
> *Their religious duties*
> *Are washed away!*
>
> *song 4*

According to the Bauls, only this path of raganuga leads to Krishna's paradise, Goloka: the eternal realm of transcendental existence beyond duality.

In Baul songs, the word raga is also used to mean the yoni, whose attribute is erotic passion. It is believed that those who travel the path of raganuga must experience and refine their passion through powerful sexual experiences. Such a path is only feasible for those who are sexually mature, because the power of passion can lead the inexperienced to unfamiliar and often frightening experiences, just as it can lead the adept to joyous ecstasy. Bauls learn sexual secrets from their gurus and practice them regularly in order to channel the sexual energy in the most positive and creative way.

Some Bauls consider vaidhi, intellectual devotion, to be an important preliminary discipline that prepares one for the overwhelming experiences of the more advanced practices of raganuga. Others see vaidhi worship as the outer expression of devotion, while raganuga is its inner form. Thus sexual practices, insofar as they are external rituals, are a form of vaidhi; but the actual sexual experience itself is raganuga, the internal form of worship.

"Another's" and "One's Own"

One of the reasons why orthodox Bengali society looks down on the Bauls is due to ignorance and misunderstanding of a fundamental concept of Baul philosophy—that of *parakiya* and *svakiya*—which is closely related to the Radha-Krishna theme. *Parakiya* literally means "another's woman," and *svakiya* means "one's own." Though sexual practices among Bauls are usually between husband and wife, both of whom have been initiated into the sexual secrets by their guru, it is not uncommon for Bauls to have more than one sexual partner. Parakiya, the taking of a sexual partner other than one's own spouse, is an ancient ideal featured in many Hindu and Buddhist Tantric schools, and particularly in the Sahajiya sect of Bengal, which has been a major influence on the Bauls.

There are three interpretations of the parakiya/svakiya concept. One is that of the apologists who, embarrassed to authorize a doctrine that seems to encourage promiscuity, explain its symbolism as follows: This life is but part of cycle of countless births and deaths. One who complacently takes this life for granted, making no effort to reach a transcendental goal, is condemned to an endless cycle of births and deaths leading nowhere. This attitude may be compared to that of a married couple who, by taking each other for granted, do not seek to extend their relationship further. This is the svakiya state of affairs. But one who has a parakiya lover is like the spiritual seeker who longs to go beyond ordinary worldly existence and dares to renounce a limited identity to become one with God.

A second explanation emphasizes the importance of the parakiya ideal to the achievement of mystical ecstasy through sexual-yogic practices. The emotions aroused in a parakiya or extramarital relationship are held to be stronger than those in a normal marriage, in which passion may be absent because of sexual incompatibility or because it has dwindled with the passage

157
◆
Part Three: The Way of Love

of time. In contrast, the close bond that exists between two lovers whose relationship is scandalous by customary social standards is seen as a more exciting, more intense form of love. When the sexual act is practiced as a mystical discipline, the more powerful the passion, the more sublime the result, for it is by the power of sexual passion that the dormant psychic energies within the body can be awakened and transmuted.

The third and perhaps most meaningful interpretation is that endorsed by the Bauls. A human being, they believe, is composed of both male and female aspects. Those with a preponderance of male elements are men, and those with a preponderance of female elements are women. Yet within every man, there is an inner woman. This is his "own," the svakiya woman. The parakiya woman is the outer, physical woman—his partner. Thus a man's parakiya lover, the "woman without," awakens the svakiya, the "woman within" himself.

Whereas the ascetic achieves divine ecstasy by arousing the dormant psychic energy (the "woman within") through yogic exercises and meditation, the Bauls awaken "her" through the passion that flows between man and woman. This process is central to the sexual practices of the Bauls, in which physical union is a preliminary step leading to advanced spiritual discipline.

The transformation from the physical to the spiritual is known as *aropa,* meaning "ascension." For the Bauls, the physical world is not something to escape from or avoid. Through enjoyment and understanding, they seek to transform the world-experience from the gross level to the subtle, from outer to inner, from material to spiritual.

> *If you don't know your "own" mind,*
> *How can you know "another's"?*
> *Knowing "another's" makes her your "own."*
> *In good faith, she will become as yours.*
> song 51

For the Bauls, parakiya and svakiya are not just metaphysical concepts—they also have a direct relevance to their daily lives. Baul sexual practices usually take place between married partners or between guru and disciple. Of course, matrimonial relationships among Bauls are quite different from the highly institutionalized marriages of Hindus and Muslims. It is not uncommon for Baul men and women to have more than one partner during their lifetime. This is partly because of their itinerant nature and partly because of the practical aspects of their sexual rites.

THE PATH OF THE
MYSTIC LOVER

The main inspiration for the parakiya ideal, as far as the Bauls are concerned, comes directly from the Vaishnava myths of Radha and Krishna. The myths depict Radha not as Krishna's wife but as either an adolescent maiden or the wife of another man. The same is true of the depiction of the Gopis, the other lovers of Krishna.

For many Vaishnavas, the emotions evoked during separation from a parakiya lover are more satisfying than those of physical union. In union, everything is still, quiet, and final, whereas separation produces a dynamic state full of anguish and anticipation. The Bauls say that those who suffer wish for God, while those who are contented rest in God.

Most Bengalis especially enjoy the Baul songs that express the extremes of emotion flowing between Radha and Krishna. Often the singers divide into two groups, one group playing the part of Radha and the other of Krishna; a kind of competition develops to see which lover will have the last word. Thus, when Radha laments, feeling betrayed, Krishna woos and extols her. He declares his remorse, but Radha, her pride hurt, shuns his advances. But how long can the lovers quarrel like this, when above all they desire to be united? Finally, Radha and Krishna surrender to each other, their pride and hurt washed away in waves of ecstatic bliss.

BECOMING A BAUL

Some are born Bauls and others become Bauls. In many ways, becoming a Baul is easier for those who are born into the tradition, because they do not have to justify their wayward and eccentric ways to their families.

A teenage Baul's mother was once complaining about her son's way-ward habits; she was worried that he was playing truant from school. In the end she gave a sigh of resignation: "Oh, well, I suppose it's in the family tradition. His father, uncle, and grandfather all ran away from home."

Newcomers may be drawn from among other wandering Bengali musicians who keep company with Bauls. They may resemble the Bauls in their outward appearance and sing similar songs, but usually they are interested only in music and, gifted with a good voice, are able to earn more

Karttik, the boy who would be Baul. Photo by Bhaskar Bhattacharyya.

money singing than by any other work. Yet through mixing with the Bauls and learning their new songs, such musicians may develop a curiosity about the Baul way and begin to seek a spiritual life.

Those who become Bauls often have to go through a traumatic period of alienation and rejection from their families. Parents and the rest of the family will do their best to dissuade their children from becoming wandering Bauls. It is difficult for family members to watch their children throwing aside their family heritage. Many children, allured by the strange and wonderful world of the Bauls, run away from the boring mundaneness of their homes.

One such case was that of Karttik, a boy of about eight who appeared just after the 1978 floods, having followed two Bauls who were returning home after a month's absence. As the Bauls' family and friends rushed to greet the pair, they noticed Karttik, lingering shyly in the background. His dark, innocent eyes appealed to them for recognition and love. The two Bauls explained that they had found the boy at a nearby town and had taken him with them after hearing from him that his parents had died and his home had been washed away.

Sympathy and pity for little Karttik was aroused among the Bauls, and one old woman took him on her lap and asked him what he planned to do or where he would go. With total assurance, the child replied: "I will become a wandering Baul."

"Can you sing?" asked one of the other Bauls.

"A little," the boy answered. After some coaxing, he picked up an ektara and, strumming it out of rhythm, began to sing in a shrill, untrained voice:

> *In this city full of labyrinths*
> *Darkness has set in the heart.*
> *What is this play of good and evil*
> *That goes on eternally?*
>
> *The rich sahib's son Donny*
> *Has untold riches;*
> *My brother Shamada has no wealth;*
> *Only the jewel of his heart.*
>
> *Some become thieves*
> *Through no fault of their own;*
> *Others become sadhus*
> *And save souls.*

I came to know Karttik quite well, seeing him turn up at various Baul gatherings, where he would display a mixture of audacity and charm. Though he could barely sing, he would often butt in while the most respected Bauls were performing. Nevertheless, he was loved and doted on by all.

About a month later, I was with a few Bauls at a small railway station when a man approached us and asked, "Have you seen a small boy traveling with Bauls?" From his description of the child, we realized at once whom he meant. We told the man Karttik's story of having lost his family in the

Bina Mai Baul encouraging the aspiring youngster. Photo by Bhaskar Bhattacharyya.

◆

floods. "Rubbish!" retorted the man. "I am his father. Karttik ran away from home a month before the floods!"

People are attracted to the Bauls' way of life for varying reasons, and not everyone who aspires to undertake their spiritual disciplines is accepted. As is quite common in India, some people may seek a religious life simply to escape the hardships of their worldly lives. Others imagine that being a Baul will mean freedom to indulge in sensual pleasures. Still others, though enthusiastic, may have unrealistic expectations of spiritual life, believing that they can achieve perfection with a minimum of effort.

A Baul guru will carefully evaluate the motivations of those who come requesting initiation. He emphasizes to the aspirant the difficulties of the spiritual path and the need for high moral standards and resilience in the face

Karttik in 1978. He is now an internationally traveled Baul. Photo by Bhaskar Bhattacharyya.

of worldly problems. He also points out that sexual practices may not be taken up until one is spiritually developed enough and has the appropriate attitude toward sex. The aspirant must understand that the Bauls do not believe in escape from worldly realities. On the contrary, they choose to enjoy the worldly life, understand it, overcome its difficulties, and eventually transcend it.

> *Life is the Shrine,*
> *The Journey and the Way.*
> *The wandering Baul is the Original One,*
> *Which only few become.*
>
> **song 1**

Those who are accepted for spiritual training undergo three stages of initiation. At each stage a guru initiates the aspirant with the appropriate mantra. Normally a different guru imparts the teachings of each stage. Although most conventional religious people in India have only one guru, the tradition of multiple gurus is a salient feature of Bengali religious life, especially among the Tantrics.

The first stage of Baul initiation is called *Pravarta* or *Diksha*, meaning "initiate." At this stage the aspirant adapts to the new lifestyle, observing and learning from the more experienced Bauls. The second stage is called *Sadhaka* or *Shiksha*. A *sadhaka* is one who practices sadhana, or active spiritual discipline; the word *shiksha* means "instruction." During this second stage the Baul embarks upon the secret sexual practices. The third stage is called *Siddha, Bheg,* or *Sannyas.* This is the stage of the Adept, when the aspirant renounces the trappings of both spiritual and material worlds, leaving the lofty heights of cosmic consciousness and returning to ordinary reality to joyfully share with others the hard-won fruits of spiritual effort.

The First Initiation

The Diksha or first initiation is symbolized by the sun, the rejuvenating principle and the power of Life. The Diksha guru is viewed as the embodiment of Krishna, for it is he who dispels ignorance and sin and sows the seed of devotion and faith.

Some Bauls receive their first initiation from Vaishnava and non-Vaishnava gurus who are not directly related to the Bauls; they often belong to more orthodox sects and may even be *brahmacharins,* whose spiritual path requires them to be celibate and observe strict orthodox codes of conduct. They don't necessarily expect their Baul disciples to follow such a path, and may be content just to see their spiritual progress.

The Diksha guru imparts the mantra that is the key to the disciple's meditation. Among Vaishnava Bauls the mantra is a combination of praises to the guru and Krishna, and Tantric "seed syllables"—monosyllabic sounds such as *Kling, Hring,* and *Sring* that, though apparently meaningless, con-tain semantic roots of deep significance. Among Sufi Bauls, the mantra is usually a chant in praise of the murshid and Allah. By repeating the Diksha mantra, the Baul fixes his mind on the object of devotion in an effort to promote the growth of Bhakti and wash away the impurities accumulated in previous lives. The mantra is likened to a lightning flash that disperses the dark clouds of ignorance. For the Bauls, faith is not a blind obsession that hides reality, but a light that illuminates reality so vividly that one is able to see its transparent nature. This light is the shrine where one takes refuge, surrendering pride, to receive freedom and grace from the "Man of the Heart."

During this first stage, newcomers decondition themselves by forgetting their old ways and learning new ones. If they come from a high caste, they must lose their sense of social distinctions and learn to live with people of all castes. If they come from a rich family, they must learn to live simply in the company of poor mendicants. Most Hindus and Muslims are strongly conditioned about social differences, religious ideas, and moral values, and it takes time for them to accept the less rigid ways of the Bauls. Freedom with responsibility is as difficult to accept and learn as restrictions, rules, and regulations.

For those who were born into the Baul tradition, this first stage is mostly a formality. Nevertheless, this first initiation is important as a psychological and spiritual transformation.

The Diksha guru often teaches breathing exercises and bodily postures in accordance with traditional yoga. These practices ensure the fitness of the body, which is vital to spiritual progress. Moreover, they relate to the central concept of Baul philosophy, that of Deha-Tattva, the Truth within the Body. The body is viewed as a shrine in which the spirit of life flows. For this spirit to flow harmoniously, the channels of energy must be free from obstruction or constriction. The degree to which physical disciplines are taught depends on the guru's knowledge of yoga and his belief in its importance. The more orthodox Vaishnava gurus place greater emphasis on Bhakti, while those with Tantric leanings stress the importance of Deha-Tattva.

The Diksha guru usually does not teach music, singing, and dancing. These arts the initiate learns in the course of his wanderings with other Bauls who sing on trains, in villages, and at festivals. Gradually the new Baul learns more songs and is able to take part in the question-and-answer repartee of the songs. Many Bauls learn to sing while very young, well before their formal initiation, so they are often accomplished musicians by the time they are adolescents.

The intellectual training of the initiates is similarly informal: They learn Baul philosophy by becoming familiar with the songs, conversing with elders, or listening to exchanges among Bauls, who often vie with each other in highly animated battles of wit. One form of communal debate is the *Doha,* which usually takes place at mealtime. One Baul will recite verses from Sahajiya poems and Baul songs that expound various aspects of their philosophy. Then another offers a reply, which either contradicts or complements the first recitation. The atmosphere of these exchanges is very informal, and there is often much humor and even the use of vulgar colloquialisms to describe the sacred tenets.

The Doha may begin with a mundane subject, such as the food the Bauls are about to eat. For example, one Baul might begin by disparaging the meal, calling it grass and water in disguise. Then another replies with a criticism of the government's food policy and racketeering among grain merchants. A third seizes the opportunity to raise the discussion to a spiritual level, using the theme of grain as a symbol of Krishna, the "seed" of love; or he might refer to gravy as a metaphor for rasa. From there the Doha proceeds to deeper philosophical themes and more complex symbolism. As can be imagined, during particularly animated exchanges, the meal is likely to take a long time, as each Baul should stop eating in order to deliver his or her recitation.

Many of the intellectual games that take place at mealtimes operate at a highly symbolic level, which may often be difficult for newcomers to understand. To the curious, the guru will explain the various meanings contained in the songs and uncover the enigmatic language at a level that corresponds to the disciple's spiritual development. If he explains too much, he is likely to endanger the progress of the disciple, who, because of lack of experience, is likely to misinterpret the teachings. This is particularly true in relation to the sexual aspects of Baul yoga.

During the Diksha stage, as indeed within every stage, Bauls are expected to fulfill the chores of everyday existence—plowing the fields, sowing and harvesting the crops, repairing the houses—and at the same time meditate on the Divine by chanting the name of Radha, Krishna, Allah, or the guru. According to the Bauls, a truly spiritual person has his feet on the ground and his head in the sky. He is as much at home in this world as in mystic trances.

> *The roots of this tree are in the sky;*
> *On the ground are its branches.*
>
> **song 64**

The Inner Practices

Whereas the Diksha stage of initiation is mainly concerned with the external aspects of being a Baul, the Sadhaka or Shiksha state, symbolized by the moon, emphasizes the subtle inner nature. The first stage prepares the mind through devotion and faith so that it can withstand, understand, and enjoy the more profound emotional and spiritual experiences of the second stage.

Many Bauls never go on to the second stage. Some are content to remain on the first level and just serve and pay homage to the Diksha guru; such people are highly regarded for having performed a noble act of humility. Others do not go on to the second stage because they are not suitably prepared for its practices of sexual yoga.

A Baul who wishes to be initiated into the second stage asks the permission and advice of the Diksha guru. If he receives permission, he must also pass muster with the Shiksha guru, who is always a married man or woman. This guru will decide whether the aspirant is psychologically and spiritually mature enough to engage in the yogic exercises and sexual rituals. Often the aspirant may be subjected to a barrage of questions about Baul customs and philosophy by a group of elders. Taunting, teasing, and insults are part of the game. If the aspirant is deemed ready to embark on this most important stage, the guru will explain the preliminaries before initiation takes place.

It is important that the aspirant be married, for the sexual practices are central to the spiritual disciplines of this stage. If not married the aspirant must find a suitable partner, sometimes with the guru's help. At times a married Baul may have to find a partner other than his or her spouse, either because the spouses have separated or because one of them is unwilling to enter the Sadhaka stage. As marriage among Bauls is a simple verbal contract and monogamy is not sacrosanct, a Baul may have more than one partner.

The Shiksha guru is regarded as an embodiment of Radha, the bliss-giving power of Krishna, for it is only she who can teach the preparation of rasa. Since Bengalis have a reputation for their insatiable appetite for sweets, it is not surprising that the Bauls often symbolize the Shiksha guru in their songs as a sweetmeat vendor or cook, patiently stirring the bubbling milk as it cooks:

> *Learn the preparation of rasa*
> *By staying with a sensual sweet-seller.*
> *Says Gosai Guru Chand to Radha Shyam:*

"Learn this song of mine.
Having created the mood
Of Krishna's paradise,
Go, obtain the nectar!"
song 31

After the Baul couple has made the symbolic offerings—fruits, grains, milk, sandalwood, tulasi beads, and flowers—to the lineage of gurus, Radha-Krishna, and other revered holy ones, the Shiksha guru initiates them by uttering the *kama-bija* mantra and the *kama gayatri*. The word *kama* means "passion," and *bija* means "seed." Kama gayatri is an invocation to the Goddess as the "passionate initiatress." Kundalini, the serpent power, is awakened by the seed of passion.

After this initiation, the Baul couple is instructed on their sadhana, both theoretically and practically. As the Bauls do not have any scriptures of their own, such teachings are transmitted directly by the Shiksha guru. Although individual gurus use their own experience to give shape and color to the teachings, the basics have remained the same for generations. The guru will quote from various religious texts to illustrate and support the teachings. Most often used are Bengali Vaishnava works, such as biographies of Chaitanya or songs and poems of Sahajiya poets such as Jayadeva and Chandidas. Gurus from the Muslim tradition may also refer to the Koran, Sufi texts, and stories about well-known Sufi saints. The more erudite gurus may quote from the Sanskrit Tantras and Hindu scriptures. Often the guru draws from "gems of wisdom" picked up from his or her own guru or from the vast body of Baul folk tales and legends. Like travelers everywhere, the Bauls are great raconteurs and gossipers, embellishing and exaggerating even the simplest incidents. Stories told around the night fire spread across the country and legends are born. In time these have formed a vast body of oral folk tales about famous and infamous Bauls, saints, and charlatans.

The initiates are instructed about breathing techniques, yoga postures, and mental control. The Bauls call their yoga the "practice of breath," for it is on the strength of breath control that the efficacy of the second stage is dependent.

Will rituals and prayers
Bring about such Union?
If so, why do yogis
Practice breath control constantly?
song 65

In yoga terminology, the art of breath control is called *pranayama*. Many people practice it in simple form as a means of relaxing the mind and body. In a sexual context, however, the techniques are much more advanced.

By "breath," the Bauls mean not simply respiration, but the vital energies that sustain life. Of these, two are of immediate importance: *apana* and *prana*. Apana is the energy that tends to move down and out of the central nervous system, pushing toward the lowest chakra, the root lotus of the sexual region. This breath is often associated with the excretory functions. Prana is the energy that moves into and up the central nervous system. Like other yogis, the Bauls believe that conscious breathing enables one to channel these two energies and thereby alter the state of consciousness.

The Baul learns to breathe in slowly and consciously through one nostril, retain the breath for a while, and then slowly release it from the other nostril. Apana is forced into the Shushumna, the central channel, through control of the lower pelvic and anal muscles, and pushed upward. The practitioner becomes more aware of sensations and movements within the body, especially during the retention of breath. Through practice, the Baul becomes able to retain the breath for longer periods—an achievement of great importance in the Bauls' yoga.

The yoga postures taught by the Baul guru are usually only those essential to keeping the body fit and flexible, and those pertinent to the sexual practices. Certain yogic exercises called *kriyas* ("actions") are also taught for this purpose. The Bauls believe that the body is a vehicle for the spirit and that it is not necessary to be a contortionist to experience the joys of life. As most Bauls come from rural areas and from relatively hard-working origins, their bodies, unlike those of rich city folks, are already lithe and strong.

Mental control is the key to the practice of yoga in its psychological aspect. The mind is made one-pointed either through the repetition of the initiatory mantra or through concentrating on the sensations produced during yoga practice. Unlike the Tantrics, the Bauls do not practice meditation involving specific visualizations.

Through inquiry and association with more experienced Bauls, some Bauls already have substantial intellectual knowledge about the Shiksha stage before entering it, for much of the information is contained in the symbolic language of the songs. However, once the Baul has received the teachings from the Shiksha guru, this information has practical relevance to the spiritual disciplines of this stage.

169

Part Three: The Way of Love

SEXUAL RITES

The main Baul sexual practices are performed in a rite that takes place during the three and a half days of the woman's menstrual period. The Baul symbolism of the "three rivers" has a practical significance here, as it refers to the three types of menstrual fluid that are secreted. Yamuna, the dark one, flows during the initial stage of menstruation, followed by Saraswati, the red fluid, and Ganga, the light-colored fluid. Each type of menstrual secretion takes 24 hours to manifest itself fully, so it is on the third "day" that the light-colored "nectar" begins to flow. During the final half day the menstrual secretion starts to ebb. The first 24-hour period is referred to as the "new" or "dark" moon, the second 24-hour period as the "first day," and the third 24-hour period as the "second day." These three 24-hour periods plus the final 12-hour period constitute the "three and one-half days" or 84 hours during which the Uncatchable can be "caught."

The following extracts from the Baul songs illustrate the sexual process.

The ebbing tide plays in three forms,
In the waters of the three rivers.

The Primordial Man has caught three forms
In the Uncatchable Moon;
He plays in the three streams,
Blending himself with the three flavors.
                                        song 80

Occasionally the three rivers,
Ganga, Yamuna, and Saraswati,
Flood down together at Triveni.

The rivers swell up
When the Three Girls play.
One is dark,
One is fair,
One is red like a ruby.

How many know of the virtues
These three girls possess?
                                        song 81

How are you going to cross that place
Where the Three Rivers meet?
Deceitful sadhus are dying at its shores!

Three Attributes form Triveni;
The three Shaktis reside there.
They manifest on the day of Union,
For the Liberation of all beings. . . .

Accomplished yogis go to the banks;
Seeing the rivers flowing,
They lose themselves in bliss.
Some are able to cross
By the strength of their practices,
While others drown.

Three Rivers combine
Into a threefold knot. . . .

song 83

Triveni, the confluence of the three "rivers," refers to the yoni, the "retort" in which the alchemy of love takes place.

The feminine "Shakti" principle in the human being is represented by Kundalini, the dynamic aspect of cosmic energy. The static aspect is the male "Shiva" principle, also known as Ishwara, the Supreme Lord. Kundalini, which rests at the root chakra, has the nature of passion and an attribute of rasa. Kundalini is visualized as a serpent-goddess coiled three and one-half times around. In men, Ishwara, who has the nature of pure love, rests calm and motionless in the thousand-petaled lotus, at the crown of the head. He cannot be recognized because he is formless. But in women, Ishwara is the Uncatchable Man, who has a playful nature and sports at the two-petaled lotus (the Third Eye). In men, rati, the calm and restful state of transformed sexual energy, has no desire for amorous love play, union, or creation.

Two implications are inherent in this. First is that in women, the Uncatchable Man, because he has the desire to play, can be tempted to "come down" to worldly reality where he can be "caught"; this is only possible in the physical body of a woman. Second, to catch the Uncatchable within oneself, Bauls teach that the mind must assume the nature of woman. An extract from a Baul song beautifully illustrates this truth:

Part Three: The Way
of Love

O mind, be like a woman!
Assuming the nature of woman,
Practice your sadhana.
The body's passion will rise.

song 41

Radha, the sensuous woman full of rasa, beckons her lover, the Uncatchable Man. Like the radiant full moon, he comes down to her abode, where the "three rivers" meet, to unite with her.

The initial stage of the sexual rite, when the dark river flows, is termed by the Bauls *amavasya,* the dark new moon.

To the one who wishes
To see the full moon
At the time of the new moon,
Lalan says:
"Always remain seated at the banks
Where the three rivers meet."

song 61

This sexual rite is also known as manifesting the full moon at the time of the new moon.

The rivers in the Bay of Bengal are tidal, and during the monsoon the high tides flood the lowlands in the estuaries and the shoals fill up with fish. Fisherman lay their nets from high bamboo structures fixed into the river bed during the low tide and wait for the sea to bring in the fish. During the ebbing tide, the fish get caught in the nets. This is a favorite image among Bengali poets and mystics. The Bauls believe that during the final state of menstruation the Uncatchable Man manifests himself in the menstrual fluid, and that to "catch" him the sadhaka has to lift him out of the "river" by yogic means.

The "Art of Archery"

The heart of the Baul sexual rite is a yogic practice symbolized as the "Art of Archery."

Having learned the Art of Archery,
Go, show your bravery in battle.

If you fight without arrows,
Your downfall will be immediate.

song 74

Kama, the Hindu Cupid, fires arrows from the bow of Rati, his consort, at the Uncatchable Man, the object of desire. The "Art of Archery" is an esoteric process by which the Bauls catch the Uncatchable Man at the seat of passion and then pull him up to the highest center of consciousness.

The Baul guru demonstrates the Art of Archery with the help of his or her partner or another experienced Baul. Even women gurus who have passed menopause demonstrate this practice. It is common for the guru and his or her partner to have sexual contact with the disciples for the first few demonstrations.

The five "arrows" of Kama are symbolic of the five rasas, the emotional stages in a relationship, and also of five yogic techniques employed during the sexual act.

Madan, the first arrow, represents rati, the ideal and final manifestation of the creative energy. *Maadan,* the second arrow, represents rasa, the dynamic creative energy. To shoot the first arrow, the man breathes in through his left nostril and the woman through her right. According to the Bauls, Madan rests in the left eye, the lunar side, for it has the calming nature of love. Through steady breathing and mindfullness, rati (which has the nature of love) is cultivated. This is *Madan kriya.* To release the second arrow, the man changes his inhalation from left to right thereby exciting the dynamic energy of erotic passion. This is *Maadan kriya.* Maadan rests in the right eye, the solar side, for it has the nature of restlessness and heat. With passion, love is awakened.

As these two arrows are being directed, the couple touch the sensitive parts of each other's bodies so as to heighten sensations. This might take the form of massage, tickling, or any kind of fondling that gives pleasure. The eight parts of the body that are specially touched are known as the eight moons: the two breasts, the two hands, the sexual organ, the navel, the back, and the face. The couple also excite each other with the play of eyes.

When the erotic energy has been sufficiently aroused, the man changes his breathing back from right to left. If, after being aroused, the man finds that he is unable to steady the sexual energy, through lack of experience or practice, he presses one heel tightly against the perineum and contracts the anal muscles, thus holding the apana breath, and at the same time turning his eyes inward and toward the Third Eye. The woman, too, concentrates all erotic energy toward the Third Eye. Through concentration on the subtle nature of sexual energy (i.e., its transformed aspect), the outer erotic energy becomes Divine, experienced within. This is known as aropa. If and when sexual energy has been steadied and the calmness of Madan descends, the couple then sexually unite. The practice of the first two arrows, Madan and Maadan, may take place also during times other than during the period of menstruation.

It is with the third arrow, *Shoshan,* that the actual yogic practice of the rites of the new moon begins to take place. With *Shoshan kriya,* love is drawn in, or absorbed, as nectar is sucked in by a bee. At this time comes the true test of yogic proficiency. Gone are all intellectual concepts and theoretical imaginings; the proof is in the rasa. The guru has taught the male disciple techniques for drawing the mixture of vaginal secretions and menstrual fluid into his lingam. Similarly, he is taught to retain his semen. This practice is similar to the Vajroli, Sahajoli, and Amaroli kriyas of the more classical schools of yoga in India.

The Uncatchable Man comes down from his abode at the Third Eye to the six-petaled lotus that "floats on the causal waters." This is "nectar that drops from the moon," known as rati. In men this nectar stays in the thousand-petaled lotus, but in women it resides at the two-petaled lotus, and during menstruation it comes down to where the three rivers meet, the yoni. Here, at the six-petaled lotus, the union of rasa and rati takes place. In women the physical manifestation of rasa is ova, and in men, semen. At the exoteric level, the union in woman is complete, for she has both rasa and rati within her body, but man has only rasa, no rati. It is for this reason that the man draws in the menstrual fluid within himself and mixes it with his rasa. Through muscular control and breathing the man is able not only to retain his semen but actually to prevent the physical manifestation of his rasa. The adept Baul is able to retain his semen, mix it with rati, and direct the sexual energy into the central nervous channel, the Shushumna. At the esoteric level, both men and women have the essence of rati within themselves, and the union is only within oneself. There is a Baul riddle that expresses the paradox:

> *The woman's period comes month by month,*
> *But tell me*
> *When does the man's take place?*

The fourth arrow is called *Stambhan,* meaning "subduing" or "holding." Love is held in a tight grasp; there is no room for anything else. This is the point when the second aropa takes place, the mystical transformation from the gross to the subtle. The rati from the physical body of the woman (parakiya) is transformed into the rati of the woman within (svakiya).

During this process the breath is held and the sexual energy is conducted into the central channel. The fiery nature of Shushumna transforms the rising passion. Time is suspended and space expanded. The couple block out their external sense perceptions, and the mind is turned inward as it experiences the world within.

This process of blocking the sense perceptions is represented in many Baul songs by the image of the nine doors or gates. They are the nine apertures of the body: the nostrils, eyes, ears, mouth, anus, and sex organ. The tenth, "hidden" gate is the aperture at the back of the throat that connects the throat to the nasal passages.

After the breath has been slowly let in through the right side, the facial apertures are closed with the fingers. The anal aperture is closed by contracting the sphincter muscles. The yoni and lingam are closed by virtue of being in union and also because of Shoshan kriya. While the breath is being retained, the tongue is turned backward to close the tenth, the "hidden," gate. The real hidden gate, however, is the entrance to the Shushumna at the root lotus. One who is able to channel the breath into it enters the world of supramundane consciousness.

As the creative energy rises, the body experiences the effects of altered states of consciousness. It trembles and perspires as the senses become acute. As this energy reaches the ten-petaled lotus, the rasa simmers. The erotic passion evaporates, swirling in the winds of prana, but love remains, gradually becoming more and more dense. In the words of the Bauls, "the milk and water separate." As the energy moves higher, unusual sounds are heard, many colors are seen, and the body experiences a sense of spacelessness. The passionate lover crosses the river by holding the breath. This is the inner journey of the lover toward the beloved. As one nears the Third Eye, a calmness descends and the body begins to feel lighter and cooler. The sensitive parts of the body start to tingle once again, and an effervescent glow seems to radiate forth.

With the fifth arrow, called *Mohan* or *Sanmohan* (meaning "eternally charmed"), all the restrained energy is finally released. This is the inner union. In the words of the Bauls, the "new moon has touched the full moon." The passionate and yearning Radha, in the darkness of the new moon, meets Krishna on the other side of the river, in his paradise, Goloka, where the light of the full moon eternally shines. This is the state of absolute bliss, the moment of total union. The man and woman are united both physically and spiritually. As breath is slowly let out, the couple lose bodily consciousness, for now they have become one and are bound in eternal ecstasy. The heat of passion has gone, the anxiety of separation is now only a dream, the delusion of the separate ego has fallen away. The transformed rasa cools in the beams of the moonlight. It becomes crystal-like, a "thousand-faced jewel" that lights up the entire universe.

> *From where does the radiant light come*
> *That shines above the two petals?*
> *Light from a jewel*
> *Bursts forth abundantly!*
>
> song 59

The Bauls call their mystical union "living death":

> *Those who have tasted the flavor of Love*
> *Have had a living death;*
> *Cured of the six ailments,*
> *Their spirit flows on.*
>
> song 52

The Four Sacraments

Having taught the Baul couple the Art of Archery, the guru explains the ritual by which the sexual practices are performed. This is sometimes referred to as the three-day rite. With the approach of the woman's menstrual period, the couple bathe and then collect flowers, fruits, grains, milk, yogurt, incense, and camphor. (However, the ritual may take place even if any of these is unavailable.) Those Bauls whose tradition requires them to recite a mantra evoke a state of calmness and one-pointedness by repeating it. They also keep a check on their diet, making sure that they are not too full, especially with heavy proteins like fish, meat, and lentils. They also avoid such "activating" foods as garlic, onion, and heavy spices.

Then, going into the privacy of their own home, the couple light a lamp fueled with ghee (clarified butter) or castor oil; put the flowers, fruits, and other offerings (including talismans from their guru and revered objects such as musical instruments) on the shrine; and light incense. Next comes the partaking of the sacraments known as the "four moons": feces, urine, menstrual fluid, and the procreative seeds (ova and semen). Among some Bauls, the last sacrament consists only of vaginal secretions.

Most people are repelled by the products of excretion. The Baul couple overcome this squeamishness by anointing parts of the body with tiny amounts of feces as a symbolic gesture. *Vivek-haldi,* the "paste of discernment," is the enigmatic term for feces in Baul songs. *Vivek* signifies the wisdom of discernment, or discrimination between the real and the unreal. Haldi is the yellow turmeric paste commonly used in Indian cooking and medicinally as a blood purifier. Since feces have the nature of earth, they are believed to possess the special power of making the body more resilient. Urine, which has the nature of water, is considered to be an antiseptic that cleans the body and rids the mind of shame.

In India, as in many other cultures, a menstruating woman is considered "unclean." Her period is regarded as a time when her body is possessed by evil spirits. According to Indian astrology, the demon Rahu swallows the moon at the time of the lunar eclipse, and the moon's dripping blood permeates the universe. It is a time for prayer and penance. It is for this reason that devout Hindus do not look at the moon during a lunar eclipse. To remove this superstitious fear, the Bauls drink a tiny amount of menstrual fluid, believing that it has the nature of fire and can help burn up the mind's impurities.

The ova and semen are generally partaken of metaphorically, by retaining them through the Art of Archery. These substances have the nature of air, for it is with "breath" that they are made to flow inward. Urine, menstrual fluid, and vaginal secretions are mixed together in a coconut bowl, sometimes together with milk, camphor, and yogurt. In another example of multiple symbolism, urine is called the river Yamuna; the ova and semen or vaginal secretions are called the river Ganga; and menstrual fluid is the river Saraswati. The following extract emphasizes the importance of these four sacraments:

> *Understand, O mind,*
> *The rites of the four moons.*
> *In observing them*
> *All suffering of the mortal body*
> *Will be overcome.*
>
> *song 73*

Having performed the ritual of the four moons, the couple proceed with the sexual practices. Since there are no authoritative scriptures or manuals regarding these practices, they are transmitted directly from guru to disciple. There are slight variations in the rituals from one group to another.

On the first day of the rite, the Bauls partake of the sacraments and release only the first two arrows. This is followed by sexual union. The yogic practices of the last three arrows are not observed at this time.

> *"New moon" is the name of this special*
>   *Union.*
> *On the first day of the waxing moon,*
> *There are no duties to be performed;*
> *It is on the second day*
> *That the spiritual rites take place.*
>
> song 78

On the second day, the sacraments are again partaken of and all the "arrows" are released. On the third day, there is no partaking of sacraments, only the releasing of the five arrows.

Having practiced for three days, the Baul couple wait for the ebbing tide, the last stage of menstruation, to catch the Uncatchable Man. This is the half-day, the final turn of the Kundalini serpent's coil. On her crown rests a jewel that she "flips with a toss of her head." All the treasures and wealth are here, for this jewel is the Man of the Heart.

> *One who manifests the full moon*
> *At the time of the new moon,*
> *Spreads joy throughout the three worlds.*
> *This rite is not for ordinary beings;*
> *On completion of it,*
> *One becomes immortal.*
> *Gosai Ramlal says:*
> *"O Gopal! You will see the Light!"*
>
> song 73

The Adept

The third and final stage of the Bauls' spiritual development is called Siddha, meaning "adept." It is also called Sannyas ("renunciation") or Bheg (the act of begging for alms). At this stage the Bauls renounce the trappings of worldly life and become mendicants. In Indian tradition, the renunciate's act of begging is seen as an act of humility. Those living on the charity of others cannot afford to be spiritually or materialistically arrogant. For every coin or grain of rice that is given, the renunciate is thankful. For the renunciate, everyone is a guru. It is with this consciousness that the sadhaka embarks on the Siddha stage.

In the Diksha stage, the guru-principle is Krishna, and in the Sadhaka stage it is Radha. Now, in the Siddha stage, the guru embodies Chaitanya. Radha and Krishna are united in the single body of Chaitanya, the androgynous aspirant who is both the devotee and the object of devotion.

In most Indian religious sects, renunciation entails the severance of family ties. One leaves home, spouse, and children to lead a life of ascetic detachment. Among the Bauls, however, usually both spouses set out on the path of renunciation together.

A Baul may also enter the stage of renunciation with a partner other than his or her spouse. Once I ran into a Baul friend whom I hadn't seen for about a year. I noticed on her forehead the mark indicating that she had taken the Siddha initiation. I knew that she was separated from her husband, whom she loved very much, and so I teasingly asked her, "Now that your husband is far away, how do you manage to keep up your practices?"

"Oh," she said, "I have a new Vaishnava for that."

"And what about your husband?" I asked.

"I entertain him when he comes," she calmly replied.

Such instances are quite common among the Bauls, especially during the third stage, when they tend to wander more and devote less time to household affairs. Although they give up their worldly life, they still continue their sexual practices—for without the sexual disciplines, a Baul would not be a Baul. The continuation of sexual activity is not in contradiction to the spirit of renunciation among the Bauls. The point is not merely to give up external things and don the garb of a renunciate, but to renounce the ego.

> *Renunciation is not cheap,*
> *To be bought by the sackload.*
> *Otherwise any thief could steal it*
> *And mutter, "Krishna, Krishna."*
>
> *song 6*

Realizing that true renunciation is internal, the Baul couple offer their worldly possessions to the Siddha guru and take to wearing a loincloth. The guru puts the mark of renunciation on their foreheads and imparts to them the initiatory mantra. Now the Baul couple have truly become crazy wanderers.

There is a stigma attached to Bauls who, having taken the second initiation of sexual practices, still end up with children. There is a sense of failure. A certain Baul had a reputation as a "fallen sadhaka," especially as he was highly regarded for his knowledge of yogic practices.

"What happened? Why could you not manage?" I asked him.

He seemed not very perturbed. "It's difficult to be a musician and at the same time to practice spiritual discipline."

"But isn't music part of your spiritual discipline?" I asked.

"Music, yes! But singing on trains, night-long musical charades, irregular meals, and that restlessness of passion that is the scourge of musicians—no! They all disturb the calmness that is essential for spiritual discipline," he replied. Then he grinned naughtily and said, "You know what happens. You can't practice your breathing regularly, and because of indulging in sensual pursuits, your rasa boils over!"

This honest statement applies to nearly all performing Baul musicians. Most of them, old and young alike, admit this incongruity, and so it is quite common for those who seek a stronger spiritual life to give up public singing.

The yogi absorbs experience and the musician expresses the spirit. Many Bauls believe that esoteric sexual practices should be embarked upon only after one has enjoyed the sensual abandon of youth.

A NIGHT OF COMMUNAL SINGING

The communal singing of the Bauls follows a traditional progression, from worldly to transcendental themes. There are four distinct stages of singing, corresponding to the stages of spiritual development. *Shtula* is the stage before a person has taken to a spiritual life; such a person is like Radha before she has seen Krishna. The next three stages correspond to the three stages of Baul initiation: *Pravarta* (or *Diksha*), the stage of initial infatuation; *Sadhaka,* the stage of endeavor; and *Siddha,* the stage of the adept, when Radha and Krishna are united.

The singing takes the form of a debate or game that provides a platform for discussions on Baul philosophy. The Bauls form into two rival groups, one assuming the role of the disciple and the other that of the guru. Questions and answers in song are exchanged until one group is unable to reply, either for lack of an appropriate response or because a statement is made that cannot be questioned. Whoever "loses" touches the feet of the opponent in the traditional gesture of respect accorded to a guru. If both groups are evenly matched, the game may go on for many hours.

Preparations are made after sunset. Lamps are lit, and the Bauls sit together in a large circle, smoking ganja, talking, tuning their instruments. The first strains of invocatory song start, gently at first, then slowly growing more impassioned as the rhythms accelerate and voices wail the names of Radha and Krishna.

To begin the debate, a Baul from one group rises and taunts the members of the rival group who are still sitting and smoking chillums (clay pipes) of ganja:

> *Know also*
> *That thousands of "mad ones"*
> *Smoking ganja endlessly*
> *Do not get anywhere!*
> > *song 7*

A glazy-eyed Baul from the rival group draws on his chillum and then stands to deliver his reply:

> *Come, come, O brothers!*
> *All who want to smoke*
> *The ganja of Love! . . .*
>
> *"Can one who smokes the ganja of Love*
> *Really get high on anything else?"*
>
> > *song 11*

Gour Khepa Baul prepares and smokes the "ganga of love." Photo by Bhaskar Bhattacharyya.

◆

With this play on words, the theme is shifted from physical to spiritual intoxication. The full moon is rising in the eastern sky, and a young Baul sings:

> *"How can I catch that moon?"*
> **song 68**

Like the moon that illumines the dark of night, Krishna, the embodiment of Love, dispels the darkness of ignorance. An old woman clad in a simple white sari picks up her cymbals and begins to express the yearning of the youthful Radha for her lover. In a shrill voice that rises to a crescendo at the end of each verse, the old woman sings:

> *When your clouds move away,*
> *The Inner Moon will appear.*
> **song 70**

The game is now at the Pravarta stage, in which the aspirant has been initiated and inspired by Krishna. As the game proceeds, the disciple group, wanting to be initiated into the second stage, asks more about the mysteries of love.

An innocent-looking young Baul with a strong but mellow voice suggests the way of the second stage:

> O mind, be like a woman!
> Assuming the nature of woman,
> Practice your sadhana.
> The body's passion will rise.
> ### song 41

Now an aged Baul in threadbare robes rises. Age and experience have taught him that the mystic must learn to see the Divine in the physical bodies of men and women before embarking on the sexual practices of the second stage. With a twinkle in his eye, he sings:

> You have not seen the living Kali
> In the midst of your home.
> Worshiping dolls and idols
> Has made you blind!
> ### song 42

The sensuous emotions having now been aroused, one of the disciple group, unable to restrain herself any longer, sings in ecstasy of the realm of sexual experience, symbolized by the ocean, the "causal waters":

> O mind, dive within and see
> The ocean of myriad forms!
> One who plunges into that ocean
> Beholds the Form behind all forms.
>
> All worldly forms are revealed
> To one who dives within. . . .
> ### song 22

A member of the guru group warns of the folly of such a reckless act for one who has not yet mastered the emotions:

Dive not into the river of passion;
You won't find its shores.
That vast river's current is strong;
It has no banks.

song 82

As the darkness of night deepens, the Bauls become more and more intoxicated, physically, emotionally, and spiritually. A young Baul continues the theme with a song about the importance of the sexual practices:

First try to discover the emotions.
Having embraced them and made love,
You will find the Jewel of Love.

song 78

A member of the guru group responds with a cautionary note:

That powerful rite
Is difficult to perform.
Only a sensuous one can know
The secret of the fluids
And the greatness of that Union.

song 79

After completing the Sadhaka stage of the singing, the two groups go on to the final stage: that of the adept. The "gurus" remind the "disciples" that they must first renounce the ego and that the external signs of renunciation are not enough. In a throaty voice that has been made even coarser by the inhalation of ganja, the old Baul in rags sings:

One does not become a renunciate
Simply by wearing beads
Or painting the forehead.

song 6

The Baul renunciate does not remove himself from the world. He lives in it, yet is above its strife, for he has found eternal joy in the bosom of the Divine Mother. He celebrates her creative potential and delights in her sportive nature. To a renunciate, everyone is the Beloved. He is like Chaitanya, the united form of Radha-Krishna, ever floating in the harmonious flow of Divine Love.

A young Baul with the mark of a Vaishnava on her forehead plucks on her two-stringed lute as she dances sensually, the bells on her feet ringing rhythmically. She sings:

> *There is no use*
> *Hiding my madness anymore;*
> *I have lost all sense*
> *Of time and space.*
> *In Bliss this mind dances;*
> *Its bells ring day and night.*
>
> > *song 3*

Night has ended, and dew drops shimmer in the early morning light. The Bauls huddle in their blankets. No one can contradict the young woman's ecstatic expression of joy, which all have shared. The game has ended.

As a warm glow appears in the eastern sky, the Bauls know that the time has come for the soaring spirit to descend, for the body to rest before rising once more to share with others the ecstasy of their Way of Love.

The old man in rags watches the other Bauls as they walk across the golden fields, back to their homes beyond the clusters of palm trees surrounding the village. Alone now, he picks up a pair of small brass cymbals and sings:

> *The light has shone in the sky;*
> *At last, compassion begins to flow.*
> *Waking up in the morning,*
> *I see before my very eyes*
> *Compassion flooding down.*
>
> > *song 44*

GLOSSARY

Advashakti (Skt) The Goddess as the primordial power that effects the creation and destruction of the universe.

Ajna (Skt) The Third Eye, the highest chakra, symbolized by a two-petaled lotus.

apana (Skt) The downward-flowing "breath" that governs the excretory functions of the body.

aropa (Skt) Transformation. The word refers to the psychological and yogic process whereby the qualities of the outer universe are transformed into the inner universe.

bhajan (Hin) A devotional song.

Bhakti (Skt) Love of God; the path of devotion and faith.

Bheg (Skt) Religious mendicancy; an act of humility that the Bauls undertake once they have received the final initiation of renunciation.

Brahma (Skt) The Creator of the universe; one of the gods of the Hindu trinity.

brahmacharin (Skt) A celibate, one who belongs to the first stage of life (*brahmacharya*) according to traditional Hinduism. Many religious people continue the practice of celibacy throughout life.

Brahman (Skt) The absolute; the Supreme Reality.

brahmin (Skt) A member of the highest Hindu caste. Traditionally, brahmins were teachers and priests. Legend says that their ancestors were born from the mind of Brahma.

Braja The region around Brindaban; the Hindu dialect spoken there is called *Brajbhasa*.

Brindaban A town south of Delhi. This is the place where, according to legend, Krishna enacted his cosmic play (*Lila*).

chakra (Skt) Literally, wheel. One of the centers of energy or consciousness in the body.

The chakras are symbolized by lotuses that "bloom" around the subtle centers of energy.

chillum (Hin) A clay pipe in which ganja is smoked.

Dasya (Skt) The second of the devotional sentiments (*rasas*); the stage of humility and service to the Divine.

Deha-Tattva (Skt) "Truth within the body"; the principle that views the human body as a microcosm.

Dharma (Skt) Righteousness; duty.

Diksha (Skt) Initiate. The first of the three stages of Baul spiritual life. Same as *Pravarta*.

Doha (Skt) Verse couplets that the Bauls recite during their communal meals.

Durga (Skt) The Goddess as the destroyer of evil and restorer of peace and harmony.

fakir (Ar) A Muslim mendicant and holy man.

Ganga (Skt) The river Ganges, one of the three holy rivers of the Hindus. As a symbol, the Ganges represents (1) the subtle channel of energy called *Ida;* (2) the flow of menstrual fluid on the last day; (3) the gross manifestation of the sexual fluids (ova and semen).

Goloka (Skt) Krishna's paradise; the eternal realm within Brindaban.

Gopi (Skt) One of the cowherding girls and women of Brindaban who were Krishna's devotees and lovers.

Gosain (Skt) A Vaishnava guru.

Hari (Skt) An epithet of Krishna.

Ida (Skt) The subtle channel of energy on the left side of the spinal cord. It has the nature of the moon because it deals with the emotional, intuitive, and reflective aspects of the mind.

Ishwara (Skt) The Lord; the Supreme Deity, unchanging and eternal. One of the names of *Shiva*.

Kali (Skt) The transcendental Goddess as the slayer of time, consciousness, and ego. She is portrayed as a dark goddess who runs amok in the cremation grounds, drinking the blood of humans (symbolizing that she is the one who absorbs all karma).

Kama (Skt) Literally, passion or lust. The name of the Hindu god of love.

karma (Skt) Action, work, duty; the law of cause and effect whereby one is responsible for one's actions, and all experience, good and bad, is the effect of actions in previous lives.

Kundalini (Skt) The dormant psychic and spiritual evolutionary power within every human being. She is symbolized by a coiled serpent that rests at the lowest chakra, the root lotus. When this "serpent" is awakened, she travels up the subtle channels of energy, opening the higher centers of consciousness.

Lila (Skt) The cosmic play or sport of Krishna in which he displays his divine qualities.

lingam (Skt) The male sex organ.

Maadan (Skt) Exhilarating and ecstatic passion. The second of the five "arrows" employed in the Bauls' sexual rites.

Madan (Skt) Love and passion. The first of the five "arrows" employed in the Bauls' sexual rites.

Madhurya (Skt) The fifth and final devotional sentiment (*rasa*); the stage of amorous, erotic love for the Divine.

Manipura (Skt) The ten-petaled lotus situated above the six-petaled lotus (Sadadal chakra). This is the chakra where the worldly realities burn away.

Mantra (Skt) A sacred syllable or phrase that is recited as a means of focusing the mind on the object of worship. A guru whispers the mantra into the disciple's ear at the time of initiation.

Mohan (Skt) Love, ecstatic enchantment. The fifth and last "arrow" employed in the Bauls' sexual rites.

Mohini (Skt) An epithet for Radha as the Enchantress.

Muladhara (Skt) The lowest chakra; the root lotus, located at the base of the spine. This center is represented by a four-petaled lotus, with the serpent Kundalini coiled up within.

mullah (Ar) A Muslim priest.

murshid (Ar) A Darbesh or Sufi guru.

paisa (Hin) A coin equivalent to one-hundredth of a rupee. (Plural: *paise*.)

parakiya (Skt) Literally, another's wife. The term refers to Tantric practices in which the sexual partner is other than one's spouse. Esoterically, it refers to the "woman without"—the physical body of woman.

Pingala (Skt) The subtle channel of energy on the right side of the spinal cord. It has the nature of the sun because it deals with the intellectual, analytical, and expressive aspects of the mind.

pir (Ar) A Sufi holy man or guru.

prana (Skt) Breath, life, vital energy. In yoga it refers to the upward-flowing "breath" that governs the inhalation and exhalation of air.

pranayama (Skt) The yogic technique of breath regulation and control.

Pravata (Skt) See *Diksha*.

raga (Skt) A mood or sentiment evoked through passion. For the Bauls, raga may refer to the yoni.

raganuga (Skt) The form of spiritual discipline in which one follows the inclinations of the heart, moved by a passionate desire to experience the grace and love of the Divine.

Rahu (Skt) The head of the mythological dragon that swallows the moon, causing the lunar eclipse. In Baul songs it is a term for the yoni.

Rama (Skt) The seventh incarnation of Vishnu and the hero of the Hindu epic the Ramayana.

rasa (Skt) Literally, juice, sap, fluid. In poetry, it is a general term for aesthetic moods. In the devotional literature of the Vaishnavas and Bauls, it refers to the five devotional sentiments known as Shanta, Dasya, Sakhya, Vatsalya, and Madhurya. Depending on the context in Baul songs, it can also refer to bodily fluids such as semen, vaginal secretions, and urine.

rati (Skt) The object of love; the Divine personified as love. When Radha is the personification of rasa, as the passionate devotee, then Krishna is the symbol of rati, the final and total experience of love. In Baul songs, rati is sometimes a term for menstural fluid.

rupee (Hin) The monetary unit of India.

Sadadal (Skt) The chakra situated at the sexual center in the body. It is symbolized as the six-petaled lotus that floats on the "causal waters."

Sadhaka (Skt) Disciple, aspirant. The second stage of Baul spiritual life, also called *Shiksha*.

sadhana (Skt) Spiritual discipline and practice.

sadhu (Skt) A Hindu holy man.

sahaja (Skt) Literally, easy, effortless. Those who follow the sahaja path are known as Sahajiyas. They believe that the ultimate reality is free, effortless, and spontaneously realized.

Sakhya (Skt) The third of the five devotional sentiments (*rasas*); the stage of loyalty and friendship toward the Divine.

samadhi (Skt) The grave or tomb of a guru or saint. The term also refers to the transcendental state in which the mind is absorbed in peace and bliss.

Sankirtan (Skt) A form of devotional worship consisting of chanting, singing, and dancing.

Sanmohan See *Mohan*.

Sannyas (Skt) Renunciation. The third stage of Baul spiritual life, also called the *Siddha* or *Bheg* stage.

sannyasin (Skt) A renunciate.

Saraswati (Skt) One of the three holy rivers of the Hindus. Also a symbol of (1) the central subtle channel of energy known as *Shushumna* and (2) the flow of menstrual fluid during the middle of the period.

Shakti (Skt) The consort of Shiva; she is his life-giving force, the dynamic energy of creation.

Shanta (Skt) The first of the five devotional sentiments (*rasas*); the stage of quietude.

Shariat (Ar) The Muslim code of law.

Shiva (Skt) The destroyer and transformer of the universe; one of the gods of the Hindu trinity. In Tantrism, he represents the transcendental experience, changeless and eternal.

Shiksha (Skt) Learning; instruction. The second stage of Baul spiritual life, during which they are taught the sexual practices. Also called *Sadhaka*.

Shoshan (Skt) To draw in. The third of the five "arrows" employed during the Bauls' sexual rites.

Shushumna (Skt) The cental subtle channel of energy in the spinal cord. It has the nature of fire because it consumes the experiences of duality which flow in the other two channels, *Ida* and *Pingala*.

Siddha (Skt) Adept. The third and final stage of Baul spiritual life, also called the *Bheg* or *Sannyas* stage.

Stambhan (Skt) To hold, grasp. The fourth of the five "arrows" employed during the Bauls' sexual rites.

Sufi (Ar) A Muslim mystic. The Sufi tradition originated in the Arab world and Persia.

svakiya (Skt) Literally, one's own wife. Esoterically it refers to the "woman within"— the dynamic power of passion.

Tara (Skt) An epithet of the goddess Kali.

Triveni (Skt) A place at Allahabad in northern India where the three holy rivers—Ganga, Yamuna, and Saraswati—merge. The confluence is also a symbol of (1) the "knots" where the three subtle channels of energy merge, at the root lotus and at the two-petaled lotus or Third Eye; and (2) the yoni, where the three menstrual "rivers" flow.

tulasi (Skt) Holy basil (*Ocimum sanctum*), a plant held to be sacred to Vishnu. Vaishnavas make their prayer beads out of its wood.

vaidhi (Skt) The form of spiritual discipline in which one follows prescribed rituals and scriptural injunctions.

Vatsalya (Skt) The fourth of the five devotional sentiments (*rasas*), the stage of parental love and affection toward the Divine.

Vedas (Skt) The authoritative scriptures of orthodox Hinduism.

Vishnu (Skt) The preserver and sustainer of the universe; one of the gods of the Hindu trinity. His devotees are known as Vaishnavas.

vivek-haldi (Skt) The "paste of discernment"; feces, one of the four ritual sacraments of the Bauls.

Viyogini (Skt) An epithet for Radha as the "separated lover" waiting for her beloved Krishna.

Yamuna (Skt) One of the three holy rivers of the Hindus; it flows near Brindaban. In Baul songs it symbolizes (1) the subtle channel of energy known as *Pingala* and (2) the flow of mentrual fluid on the first day of the period.

yoni (Skt) The female sex organ.

THE PATH OF THE
MYSTIC LOVER

BIBLIOGRAPHY

Attar, Farid al-Din. *Muslim Saints and Mystics,* tr. A. J. Arberry. Chicago: University of Chicago Press, 1966.

Bagchi, P. C. "Caryagiti-Kosa of the Buddhist Siddhas." *Visvabharati Quarterly,* 1956.

Banerjee, A. C. *Guru Nanak and His Times.* Punjab University, 1971.

Banerjee, Akshaya Kumar. *Philosophy of Gorakhnath.* Gorakhpur, 1961.

Banerji, P. K. "Sandhya Bhasa." *Visvabharati Quarterly,* 1956.

Basham, A. L. *The Wonder That Was India.* Fontana Ancient History, 1971.

Basu, M. M. *Dina-Chandidaser Padavali.* Calcutta University, 1935.

———. *Sahajiya Sahatiya.* Calcutta University, 1932.

———. *The Post-Chaitanya Sahajiya Cult of Bengal.* Calcutta, 1930.

Bhandarkar, Sir R. G. *Vaishnavism, Saivism and Minor Religious Systems.* Poona, 1929.

Bhattacharyya, Benyotosh. *An Introduction to Buddhist Esoterism.* London: Oxford University Press, 1932.

———. *Tantric Cults Among Buddhists.* Vol. 2, *Cultural Heritage of India.* Calcutta: Ramakrishna Mission, 1950–1960.

———. "The Buddhist in Bengal." *Dacca Review,* 2 (1921).

Bhattacharyya, Deben. *Mirror in the Sky.* London: George Allen & Unwin, 1974.

———. *Love Songs of Chandidas.* London: George Allen & Unwin, 1967.

Bhattacharyya, Upendranath. *Banglar Baul O Baul Gan.* Calcutta: Orient Book Co., 1971.

Chakravarti, Chintaharan. "Antiquity of Tantricism." *Indian Historical Quarterly* (Calcutta), 4 (1930).

Chatterji, S. K. *The Origin and Development of the Bengali Language.* London: George Allen & Unwin, 1979.

Chaudhuri, Roma. *Sufism and Vedanta.* 2 vols. Calcutta, 1945–1948.

Das, Sricharan. *Tattvarasamrit Jnanmanjari.* Calcutta, 1976.

Dasgupta, S. B. *Obscure Religious Cults as Background of Bengali Literature.* Calcutta, 1962.

———. *Sri Radhar Kramavikasa.* Calcutta: A. Mukherji & Co.

Dasgupta, S. N. *Yoga as Philosophy and Religion.* London: Kegan & Paul, 1924.

Dimock, Edward. *The Place of the Hidden Moon.* Chicago: University of Chicago Press, 1966.

De, S. K. *The Early History of the Vaishnava Faith and Movement in Bengal.* Calcutta: Firma K. L. Mukhopadhyay, 1961.

Douglas, Nik, and Penny Slinger. *Sexual Secrets: The Alchemy of Ecstasy.* Rochester, Vt.: Destiny Books, 1979.

Edgerton, F. "Prana and Apana." *Journal of American Oriental Society,* 78 (1958).

Eliade, Mircea. *Yoga, Immortality, and Freedom.* New York: Pantheon, 1958.

———. *The Sacred and the Profane.* New York: Harper, 1959.

Fatemi, Nasrollah, Farmarz, and Fariborz. *Sufism.* Cranbury, N.J.: A. S. Barnes & Co., 1976.

Ghosh, Sishir Kumar. *Lord Gouranga.* Calcutta, 1923.

Goswami, B. K. *The Bhakti Cult of Ancient India.* Varanasi: Chowkahamba, 1965.

Goswami, Rupa. *Ujjvala-Nilmani.* Bombay: Kavyamala Press, 1913.

Guenther, Herbert V. *The Royal Song of Sahara.* Shambhala, 1973.

Kabir, Humayun. *Islam in India.* Vol. 4, *Cultural Heritage of India.* Calcutta: Ramakrishna Mission, 1956.

Kaviraj, Gopinath. *Guru Tattva O Satguru Rahasya.* Calcutta: Sri Krishna Sangha, 1967.

Kingsland, Kevin and Venika (trans.). *Hathayoga Pradipika.* England: Grael Communications, 1977.

Krsananda Agamvagisa. *Tantrasara.* Basumati Press, 1929.

Machwe, Kabir. *Kabir.* Delhi: Sahitya Akademi, 1968.

Majumdar, R. S. *Advanced History of India.* London, 1950.

Mukhopadhyay Harekrishna. *Vaishnava Padavali.* Calcutta, 1971.

Nicholson, R. A. *Studies in Islamic Mysticism.* Cambridge, 1967.

———. *Rumi: Poet and Mystic.* London: George Allen & Unwin, 1964.

O'Flaherty, Wendy. *Asceticism and Eroticism in Mythology of Siva.* London, 1973.

Orr, W. G. *A Sixteenth Century Indian Mystic.* London: Lutterworth Press, 1947.

Owen Cole, W. *The Sikhs.* London: Routledge Kegan & Paul, 1978.

Ray, Sukmar. *Music of Eastern India.* Princeton, 1957.

Scott. "Kabir, Maverick and Mystic." Ph.D. thesis, University of Wisconsin, 1976.

Sen, Dinesh Chandra. *History of Bengali Language and Literature.* University of Calcutta, 1954.

Shastri, Haraprasad. *Bauddha Gan O Doha.* Calcutta University, 1917.

Snellgrove, D. L. *Hevajra Tantra.* 2 vols. London, 1959.

Singer, Milton (ed.). *Krishna Myths, Rites and Attitudes.* Honolulu: East West Center, 1965.

Singh, Kushwant. *History of the Sikhs.* London: Oxford University Press, 1966.

Swami Bhakti Hrdya Bon Maharaj. *Bhaktirasamrita Sindhu of Rupa Goswami.* Brindaban.

Vasu, Rai Bahadhur Srisa Chandra. *The Siva Samhita.* Orient Reprint, 1975.

Vaudeville, Charlotte. *Kabir.* New York: Oxford University Press, 1974.

Woodroffe, John. *Tantrik Texts; Shakti and Shakta; Serpent Power; Principles of Tantra.* Madras: Ganesh.

INDEX

*Numbers in **bold italic** indicate photographs and illustrations*